STAIRWAY WALKS in LOS ANGELES

Adah Bakalinsky
and
Larry Gordon

WILDERNESS PRESS
BERKELEY

FIRST EDITION 1990
Copyright © 1990 by Adah Bakalinsky and Larry Gordon

Drawings by Trudie Douglas
Maps by Pat Beebe
Book Design by Roslyn Bullas
Cover Design by Larry Van Dyke

Library of Congress Card Catalog Number 90-41027
International Standard Book Number 0-89997-112-1

Manufactured in the United States of America

Published by   Wilderness Press
                     2440 Bancroft Way
                     Berkeley, CA 94704
                     (415) 843-8080
                     Write for free catalog

Library of Congress Cataloging-in-Publication Data

Bakalinsky, Adah.
    Stairway walks in Los Angeles / Adah Bakalinsky and Larry Gordon.— 1st ed.
       p. cm.
    Includes index.
    ISBN 0-89997-112-1 (Pbk.)
    1. Los Angeles (Calif.)—Description—1981- —Tours.   2. Walking—California—Los Angeles—Guide-books.   3. Architecture—California—Los Angeles—Guidebooks. 4.   Stairs—California—Los Angeles—Guide-books. I. Gordon, Larry, 1952- .   II. Title.
F869.L83B35   1990

DEDICATION

To Leda and Elizabeth with love.
—Larry

To My Los Angeles Aunts:
Aunt Sarah, the California pioneer in my family who came to the city in 1937 for a two week visit and decided to stay. In appreciation for her kindess and expertise that kept me in custom-made dresses until I was 13. Aunt Raye, in appreciation for her generosity in giving up her Saturday afternoons to take me to the movies and vaudeville shows at the old Orpheum Theater in St. Paul.
—Adah

FOREWORD

by Ernest Callenbach

Walking in *Los Angeles*? The place where science-fiction writer Ray Bradbury reported being accosted by police simply for the suspicious act of being a pedestrian?

Well, yes. Adah Bakalinsky and Larry Gordon have done a lot of walking in Los Angeles, and they are still at large—even though they must arouse some suspicion by taking notes as they walk.

In this book, following the kind of little-known stairways that Los Angeles and a few other wonderful cities have, they let their curiosity lead them to fascinating places that the ordinary visitor, or for that matter the freeway-confined Angeleno, never hears about, much less sees—and still less comes to know and appreciate.

Walking with their book in hand is like walking with a lively and perceptive aunt who's always full of historical asides and startling bits of current information. They have an eager eye for landscape perspectives, remarkable old (or new) buildings, ironwork decorations, flowers and other plants, and relics of the movieland past. Above all they give us a sense of lived-in *neighborhoods* in a city usually thought of as completely dominated by cars.

In a car, no one is a citizen—just a driver, passing through, showing no curiosity, taking no responsibility. Adah Bakalinsky's and Larry Gordon's passionate, gossipy interest in how and where people live, and in the ways they shape their physical environment, shows the way to an opposite and healthier attitude. On foot, people *care* about their physical world. So let this charming guide lead you through the byways of Los Angeles and also into a new way of looking at cities everywhere.

PREFACE

I, Adah, am a San Franciscan, not by birth, but by inclination and residence.

I, Larry, born in New Jersey, live in Los Angeles by virtue of work and wife's family ties. Being curious, I explore my environment, always looking for the lively walking streets of the sort I remember from the east.

So together we are writing about an aspect of Los Angeles disregarded by most residents and visitors—its outdoor stairways! Los Angeles has more than 200 stairways; they qualify Los Angeles as a walking city.

To walk the neighborhoods is to see and understand the essence of Los Angeles. Neighborhoods are the backbone from which the color, the diversity, the strength and the energy special to L.A. emanate—neighborhoods not far from the famous corner of Hollywood and Vine, or the famous shopping strip on Rodeo Dr. in Beverly Hills; neighborhoods where roses grow wild, nasturiums twine around the porches, containers of cacti overflow the solariums, and neighbors decide how to landscape a common stairway.

Los Angeles stairways exhibit great variety. Some are easily seen, some hidden; some are short, some extraordinarily long. They are constructed of a variety of materials including brick, wood and cement. Some provide a shortcut to spiraling up a hill; some lead to a cul-de-sac. And when you walk on a stairway it allows a changing landscape to come into view.

Walking the stairways in Los Angeles provides a good introduction to unofficial and folk history of the neighborhoods. The stairways become informal "parlors" where one can easily visit with the locals, or merely give a friendly greeting. Los Angeles is one of a small number of American cities, including San Francisco, Pittsburgh, Berkeley and Bisbee, Arizona with numerous stairways, the human-scaled urban artifacts that encourage walking and talking, marks of a civilized city.

Contents

Foreword by Ernest Callenbach
Preface
Contents
Introduction

Los Angeles: In the Beginning   *1*

Chapter   THE WALKS
1   **Downtown:** The Cradle for the City of Angels   *5*
2   **El Sereno:** Not Even the Natives Know About This   *12*
3   **Highland Park:** Avenue, Lane, Street, Place and Drive   *15*
4   **Mt. Washington East and West:** An Articulated Walk   *21*
5   **Echo Park:** Gingerbread Houses and Sports Stars   *29*
6   **Elysian Heights:** Memorial to a Cat Named Room 8   *35*
7   **Southwest Silver Lake:** Above the Blue Waters with Laurel and Hardy   *39*
8   **Eastern Silver Lake:** The Streetcar Doesn't Stop Here Anymore   *43*
9   **Franklin Heights:** Detours, Uphills and No Sidewalks   *47*
10   **Los Feliz:** Eclecticism Works if All Is in Scale   *53*
11   **Lower Beachwood:** Churches, Temples, Monasteries and Mosques   *58*
12   **Upper Beachwood:** Castles in the Shadow of the Sign   *63*
13   **Whitley Heights:** Beautiful and Besieged   *67*
14   **High Tower:** Holly, Stars and Visions   *70*
15   **UCLA:** Treeing Around the Campus   *75*
16   **Venice:** *Divertissement*—Beware the Mallard Doo   *83*
17   **Santa Monica:** Sea Breezes and Clean Air, but Watch for Street Angles   *89*
18   **Castellammare:** Washout/watchout   *95*

Acknowledgments   *100*

Index   *101*

INTRODUCTION

Notes From My Journal:
L.A. Pop. 3,000,000. L.A Longitude: 118° 5'W. L.A. Latitude: 34°3'N. L.A. 465 square miles.

Our mission: to cajole, to attract, to entice people to walk in the neighborhoods. By crossing freeways and hills, we discover neighborhoods within short distances of our homes. Within the neighborhoods we find "pedestrian friendly" walks, containing cul-de-sacs, disconnected streets with the same name, streets with different names that curve into each other and of course stairways, all providing interest and variety to the walker. Stairways, our favorite nonconforming urban form, are the focal points of our 18 neighborhood walks.

> Walks are graded in terms of the energy obtained by eating oranges. A two-orange walk is our baseline, a moderate walk. An orange plus other suggested edibles indicates a moderate-plus walk. The time needed per walk is around 2- 2 $\frac{1}{2}$ hours.

The descriptions in the chapters were up to date at publication time. However, neighborhoods evolve continually, as we discovered in rescouting our routes. Some stairways may have gates, and gates may be locked. A natural phenomenon, like a mud slide, may close off a path. If the way is blocked, find a detour, and re-connect with our route as soon as you can.

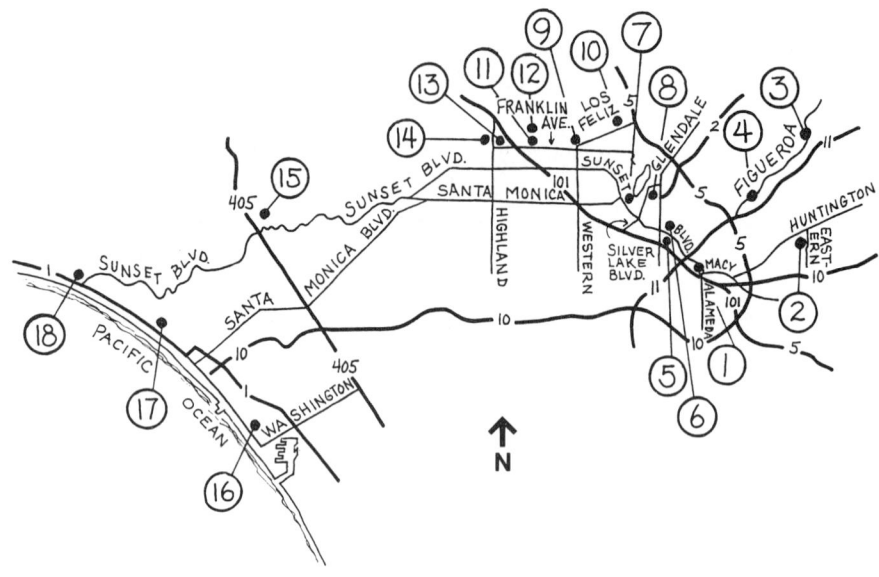

KEY TO LOS ANGELES MAP

1 — Downtown
2 — El Sereno
3 — Highland Park
4 — Mt. Washington
5 — Echo Park
6 — Elysian Heights
7 — Southwest Silver Lake
8 — Eastern Silver Lake
9 — Franklin Heights
10 — Los Feliz
11 — Lower Beachwood
12 — Upper Beachwood
13 — Whitley Heights
14 — High Tower
15 — UCLA
16 — Venice
17 — Santa Monica
18 — Castellammare

LOS ANGELES
In the Beginning

I wish I had been present the August week of 1769 when Father Juan Crespi and Captain Gaspar de Portola and their party of 67 men arrived from Mexico and camped near what is now the hub of Los Angeles.

In his journal, Father Crespi wrote, "We entered a very spacious valley, well-grown with cottonwoods and alders among which ran a beautiful river from north-northwest, and then doubling the point of a steep hill [now Elysian Park] it went on afterward to the south..this plain where the river runs is very extensive. It has good land for planting all kinds of grain...and is the most suitable site of all we have seen for a mission, for it has all the requisites for a large settlement." The next day's entry notes, "...after crossing the river, we entered a large vineyard of wild grapes and an infinity of rosebushes ...all the soil is black and loamy and is capable of producing every kind of grain and fruit which may be planted."

The Spaniards encountered the Gabrielino Indians, who lived near the Los Angeles River in one of 28 Indian villages that existed in what is now Los Angeles County, and zealously undertook the task of converting them to Christianity.

In anticipation of a pueblo's being established, the families of soldiers and colonists came up from Mexico, and on September 4, 1781, Los Angeles—El Pueblo Nuestra Senora de la Reina de los Angeles de Porciuncula—was formally established by Don Felipe de Neve, the first Spanish governor of the Californias. The population was 44.

1800. The population of El Pueblo is heterogeneous—Mestizos, Spaniards, mulattoes, Indians and Blacks, numbering approximately 300.

The Californias are a dubious acquisition for the Spanish. The number of conversions is limited, and the army and the crown have a short attention span when they do not smell gold or spices. Consequently, there is minimum interference from Spain.

1822. Spanish rule comes to an end. California is now part of the United Mexican States, and the missions become secularized. Land grants are common gifts to family and friends. Dona Vicente Sepulveda, one of a group of 66 women grantholders in Southern California, is recognized as a very capable and important ranchera for three decades.

1842-45. Power struggles ensue. Pio Pico, California born, revolts from the restraints of the governing body in Monterey. Governor Manuel Micheltorena and his gang of recidivists, a.k.a. police, arrive to destroy Pio Pico. They fail. Pico is victorious at the Battle of Cahuenga Pass, and he becomes governor.

August 1846. The American flag flies over Los Angeles, population 2500. Although there is no resistance initially, a change of American military leadership precipitates a Mexican revolt here which continues for three months. Commander Stockton and General Kearny recapture Los Angeles on January 10, 1847. Captain John C. Fremont meanwhile draws up a personal treaty of surrender for Andres Pico and his rebels, to occur the following day, January 11. Fremont defies General Kearny, and decides to be governor. His hubris is rewarded by a court-martial in 1848.

1850. Los Angeles is incorporated under American rule, and the state of California is admitted to the Union on September 9, 1850.

1857. Lieutenant Edward O.C. Ord completes the first survey of Los Angeles, establishing the present street pattern. An appeal is made to the general public to purchase land at $1.00 an acre.

1876. The transcontinental railroad accelerates the influx of people into Los Angeles. During the railroad rate war, it costs $5 to come to Los Angeles from the Midwest. In the 10-year period 1880-1890 the population increases from about 11,000 to about 50,000.

1893. The discovery by E.L. Doheny of a major oil field in Los Angeles is the beginning of the oil boom and of the change in transportation patterns from railway to automobile.

1901. The Pacific Electric Railway Company articles of incorporation are signed. "Safety, Efficiency, Speed"—the motto of the PE—accurately describes the most perfect electric-railway system in the world, according to everyone who rides the interurban red cars regularly. Los Angeles residents feel they are living in nirvana. Why wouldn't they write home and "P.S. come on down"? By 1910 the population was near 320,000.

1913. This is the infamous year that water, wrested and stolen from Owens Valley, is delivered, quenching Los Angeles thirst and ending any doubts about the power of the big city. The Owens Valley farmers are left in desperate straits; the San Fernando Valley, recipient of much of the excess water, blossoms, and is annexed to Los Angeles in 1915. The population continues upward.

1920s. Movies become a major industry. Hollywood is the favorite location for studios; movie stars' salaries become astounding—Gloria Swanson's is $20,000 per week.

1930s. These are the years of natural disaster—severe drought and depression; the Long Beach 6.3 magnitude earthquake of 1933; and the record flood of March 1938. The earthquake leads to passage of the Field Act, which mandates earthquake-safety codes for public-school buildings in California.

1940s. World War II. Industrial development is encouraged; freeway development begins. Automobiles bring people to their destinations faster and faster, but not so fast that they don't begin to notice—smog.

1950s. The air-pollution control district bans residential incinerators. Los Angeles repeals the height law restricting buildings to 150 feet, opening the way for high-rises. The mayor succeeds in enticing the Dodgers away from Brooklyn, making Los Angeles a major-league city.

Notes From My Journal:
Lewis Mumford wrote after World War II that "Central Los Angeles is occupied by streets, freeways, parking facilities and garages." On the other hand, Anais Nin wrote in the 1950s that she found Los Angeles to be the most stimulating city of new ideas and talented people outside her native Paris!

1960s. Urban-renewal projects begin. In August 1965 the Watts racial riot in southeast Los Angeles breaks out. It lasts four days and nights and focuses nationwide attention on the poverty-stricken area and on the paucity of social services available to its residents.

1970s. Another riot, protesting the Vietnam war and the inequities in services available to the Chicanos living in East Los Angeles. Thomas Bradley, the first black mayor of Los Angeles, is elected in 1973.

To the present. Highrises outline the horizon; Los Angeles has become international corporate headquarters for finance, manufacturing, shipping and retailing companies—especially Pacific-rim companies. A sustaining interest in the arts is evidenced by the new museums, theaters and art galleries. Los Angeles still retains a principal position in movie and TV production.

Thousands of refugees from Latin America and the Orient pour into L.A., and bring vitality and diversity of cultures—but also problems of housing, transportation, education, environment and crime.

The city that so many people think is synonymous with automobiles may even now be reverting to the days of the trolley. Union Station, which is very close to where Father Crespi camped in 1769, will be the hub of a new subway and light rail system. Perhaps this is a shift in transportation and commuting patterns that indicates the beginning of a new cycle of L.A. history.

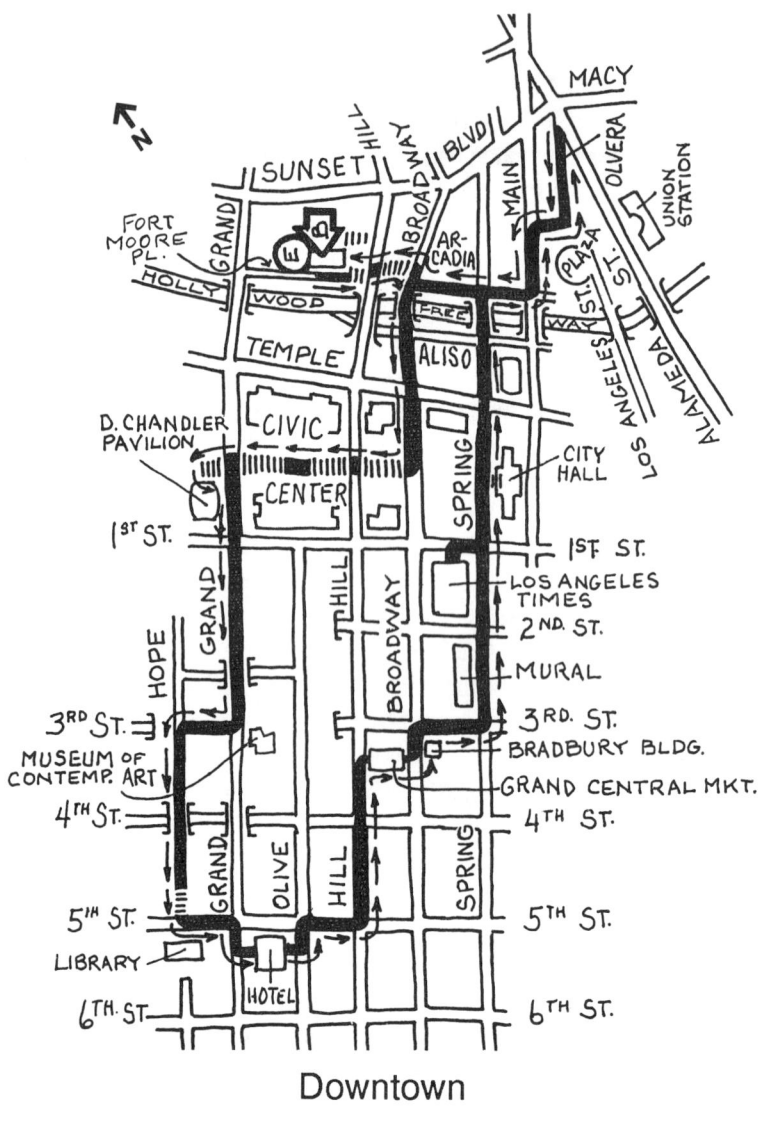

Downtown

Walk 1

DOWNTOWN
The Cradle for the City of Angels

Boundaries: Hope St., Sunset Blvd., Main St., Fifth St.
Rating: 3 Oranges

■ Downtown Los Angeles may not be the neighborhood most tourists clamor to see; it may not even be regularly visited by most natives in this sprawling megalopolis of enclaves and freeways. But downtown is the city's birthplace and is still the heart of finance, law, government, journalism and, more recently, the arts. Plus, there are the thriving ethnic communities of Chinatown and Little Tokyo for strolling and dining and the enormous discount garment and jewelry districts for shopping.

■ Most of the stairways in downtown go up and down Bunker Hill, a steep rise above Broadway that once was the most fashionable neighborhood. But time and wealth marched on, leaving the huge collection of Victorian homes to decay and, later, eventual demolition in a controversial 1960's urban renewal project. The result is a new Bunker Hill seemingly weighted down with office skyscrapers and condominium projects but also graced with new cultural landmarks. So, within one walk, a visitor can taste the early days of Los Angeles as well as what its boosters hope will be its future as the capital city of the Pacific Rim.

■ We start at the Fort Moore Pioneer Memorial, which fronts Hill Street, north of Temple St. between the Hollywood Freeway and Sunset Blvd., an easy walk from most downtown bus lines and Civic Center parking lots.

Fort Moore Pioneer Memorial

■ By car, two other suggestions: 1) If heading downtown on Sunset Blvd., watch for the right turn onto Hill St., just after Grand, and the memorial is just after the curve of Hill St.; there is street parking during non-business hours. 2) Or, park in one of the Music Center lots on Grand St. between Sunset and Temple, and then walk the block over the Hollywood Freeway toward Sunset, looking for the street sign for Fort Moore Pl., which is also the main entrance to the headquarters for the Los Angeles Unified School District; turn right down Fort Moore Pl., passing the yellow one room school house (built in 1876 and moved here as an information center) in the courtyard, until the road curves to the left. The top of the two stairways will be there—beneath the beautiful Ficus Retusa trees across from the front of the school board complex. Descend one of the stairways

■ The Fort Moore Pioneer Memorial is a large, hillside complex of fountains, flagpoles and bas relief sculptures honoring a Mormon battalion's exploits in the War with Mexico. (If you arrived on Hill Street, ascend one of the memorial's stairways and descend the other.) From its top are great views of downtown and the various modes of transportation that built L.A.: the Los Angeles River (now a concrete-sided stream), the great train yards and the roaring freeways. Straight ahead are the half-Moorish, half-Art Deco style Union Station and the Post Office depot. At the base of the memorial, we are on Hill St. After reading the inscriptions honoring the soldiers, we cross Hill at the crosswalk at the edge of the monument closer to the Hollywood Freeway and take the utilitarian concrete stairway, flush against the freeway, down to Broadway, turn right and continue on Broadway just past Temple Street.

■ On our right will be the Hall of Records, designed by Richard Neutra and finished in 1962. In view on our left will be the main entrance of the majestic City Hall. Just after the Hall of Records on Broadway, in line with City Hall, is the double-sided stairway entrance to the Civic Center Mall. A series of easy steps leads us up to the Court of Historical Flags, lined with banners from the Revolutionary War. Watching for possible subway construction detours, we cross Hill Street and follow pedestrian pathways on either side of the circular driveway going to a subterranean garage. Continuing straight ahead, we are in a park between government buildings. On one side is the county courthouse, on the other is the county Hall of Administration. Along the central lawn are statues of George Washington and Christopher Columbus. And, we walk up one of the twin stairways up to the monument dedicated to Ukranian victims of oppression under Stalin and Hitler. At the foot of another set of twin stairs are a large fountain and large plaque and map detailing the settlement of the city. We ascend the stairway. (Or we can take the pedestrian tunnel under Grand Ave.)

■ On top, we cross Grand Avenue to the low-riser steps up to the plaza of the Music Center, the cultural focus of downtown. Here are the Dorothy Chandler Pavillion (home of the Philharmonic and the Academy Awards), the Ahmanson Theater and the Mark Taper Forum. We can explore the center's plaza and return down the stairway back to Grand and turn right. We cross Grand at the first corner, which is First St. On that corner is a handsome bust of Abraham Lincoln. Continuing on Grand, we now cross First St. On the other side of Grand is a parking lot which will one day be the site for the new home for the Los Angeles Philharmonic being built with donations from the Walt Disney family.

■ We continue along Grand, heading toward the skyscrapers of the still-unfinished redevelopment project on Bunker Hill. But just before Third Street is great relief: the red-sandstone facade of the new Museum of Contemporary Art, a 1986 cluster of austerely beautiful low-rise structures designed by Arata Isozaki and praised as a work of art in its own sake. At the rear and side are peaceful gardens, with fountains and a patio cafe.

■ From the front of the museum, we cross Grand at Third and continue on Third Street one block and turn left on Hope St. On Hope, we are in the center of West Coast corporate power. The names on the buildings tell the story: Wells Fargo, Security Pacific, Arco, First Interstate. The Wells Fargo Court at #330 Hope has some nice restaurants, including a fancy McDonald's. We continue on Hope, passing the glass and green-paneled YMCA on the right.

■ At the end of Hope, on our left is the highest building in the city: the 73-story First Interstate World Center, called Library Tower by many. Just next to that tower is what city planners hope will become the most famous stairway in Los Angeles; some go as far as to say it will become the equivalent of the beloved Spanish Steps in Rome. Finished in 1990, the Bunker Hill Steps were designed by renowned landscape architect Lawrence Halprin. A miniature river of bubbling water gushes down the center and shops and cafes are scheduled to open on the terraces.

■ As we descend the stairway, the sunburst-gold pyramid top of the Central Public Library will be directly ahead, across Fifth St. The 1925 masterpiece of architect Bertram Goodhue, the library is a mixture of

Egyptian and other styles. The library is being renovated and expanded—a job hastened by the tragic arson fires of 1986. Meanwhile, we can content ourselves by reading the inscription carved into the library directly ahead of us at the bottom of the Bunker Hill Steps: "Books alone are liberal and free. They give to all who ask. They emancipate all who serve them faithfully."

■ We turn left on Fifth and continue on Fifth. (For an interesting detour, we cut to the other side of Fifth, along Grand Ave., is the new main entrance to the recently refurbished Biltmore Hotel. We can cut through the hotel, peeking into its lobbies and ballrooms. We exit via the Olive St. side of the hotel along Pershing Square. Outside the hotel, we turn left and walk along Olive to the corner and turn right on Fifth.)

■ We continue on Fifth and cross Hill St. and turn left on Hill. We follow Hill, but beware of subway construction. Between Third and Fourth, we will pass near the spot where a funicular, the beloved Angel's Flight, once took as many as 12,000 riders a day up the 325-foot-long incline for a nickel; built in 1901, Angel's Flight was closed in 1968 in the name of what I feel is questionable progress, replaced by a housing project. That created a real problem for pedestrian access up steep Bunker Hill and city planners promise a new funicular will be built nearby in a few years.

■ On Hill, just before Third Street is the entrance to the Grand Central Market. We turn right into the market hall. Built in 1917, the Market is an enormous Old World collection of fruit stands, butcher shops and bakeries. It has a strong Latin flavor and an emphasis on the inexpensive. We can eat and browse our way through to the Broadway entrance and turn left. We will pass the Million Dollar Movie Theater, a Spanish language cinema housed in one of the ornate movie palaces that made Broadway Los Angeles's premier street in the Twenties and Thirties. Broadway is still a bustling shopping and entertainment area, primarily for Latino immigrants. We cross Broadway at the corner of Third St. and on the other side, at #304 Broadway, is the Bradbury Building, an 1893 landmark which has one of what I think is the most beautiful interiors in L.A. Behind the bridal shop at street level is a serene court surrounded with Victorian grillwork, dark wood and antique elevators—all under a dramatic skylight. Going inside is like taking a step back into a gentler time; quite a contrast to the bustle outside.

■ We return to Third St. and continue one block to Spring St. Turn left on Spring. On our left, in the middle of the block, we can study the bas relief sculpture of the history of journalism on the Los Angeles Times garage built in 1989. We stay on Spring, crossing Second St. and there is the Art Deco-style Times complex, stretching along Spring to First. This block once contained the first brick school house in the city, the first city hall and even a Civil War era army corral that held camels.

■ We turn left on First Street and the main lobby of the Times is just up from the corner. The lobby, called the Globe lobby after its centerpiece globe of the world spinning around an astrological belt, has interesting exhibits on the city's history and journalism. The strong Art Deco flavor extends even to the bronze mailboxes; it feels like a place where Clark Kent would work. Tours of the building can be arranged from here. This is actually the fourth home of the Times; one of the predecessors was blown up in a 1910 labor dispute.

■ We return to Spring St., cross it and turn left, crossing First St. Just ahead on Spring is City Hall, at #200 Spring St. We walk up its temple-like courtyard steps to the entrance of the 28-story tower, which was built in 1928 and was the highest structure in the city until the 1950's. Tours are available as is an elevator ride up to the observation deck.

■ Back down the steps to Spring St., we turn right and continue on Spring, crossing Temple. The U.S. Court House is on our right. On Spring, we cross first Aliso St., then over the Hollywood Freeway to Arcadia St. Here some walkers may wish to return to the starting point. If so, turn left on Arcadia and follow it to Broadway. Cross Broadway, and on the right side will be the concrete stairway leading back to Hill St. and the Fort Moore Memorial.

■ However, for those interested in seeing the old heart of Los Angeles, what was the 18th Century El Pueblo de Los Angeles, we turn right on Arcadia and follow it, paralleling the freeway for one block. Then, we turn left on Main St. 400 N. At #535 Main St. is the historic Church of Our Lady the Queen of Angels, the soul of Catholic Latino life in L.A. It was completed in 1822, although its present facade dates to 1861.

■ Just after the church on Main is a crosswalk. We cross Main there to the pedestrian plaza ahead. We are in the El Pueblo State Historical Park, site of the founding of the city in 1781 and a repository of Mexican heritage. (Free guided tours of the park are offered Tuesday-Saturday, 10 A.M.- 1 P.M. hourly from the Hellman building next to the firehouse at the southeast corner of the plaza. For more information, call 213-628-1274.)

■ On our left is the entrance to Olvera St., a reconstruction of a Mexican colonial market street. Stalls and shops sell artifacts and sweets while cafes beckon with tacos and musical serenades. It may have an air of tourism kitsch, but the auto-free environment is a pleasure. We walk down to its end and back up. At #8 Olvera St., is the Avila Adobe, the oldest existing house in the city; it was built in 1818 by Don Francisco Avila, one of the city's leaders, and it served briefly as American headquarters during the War with Mexico.

■ (As we emerge back to the plaza, the Union Passenger Terminal, the glorious railroad station finished in 1939, will be over our left shoulder across Alameda St. It is worth a detour for those with the time.)

■ From Olvera St., we cross the plaza, past the bandstand in the center. On the other side is a pedestrian street called Paseo de la Plaza. To the left, where it intersects with Los Angeles St. is a restored firehouse, dating back to 1884. Next door, at #130 Paseo de la Plaza is the park office. At the corner of Main, at #430, is the Pico House, a former hotel built by the last Mexican governor of California in 1869. The Italianate building is now used as an art gallery. We turn left on Main, following the exterior of the Pico House. At #416 Main is the first Masonic Hall in Los Angeles, from 1858.

■ We turn right at the corner of Arcadia, cross Main, and continue on Arcadia paralleling the freeway. We stay on Arcadia, crossing Spring and Broadway. On the other side of Broadway, just to the right of the corner, is the concrete stairway up to Hill St. and the Fort Moore Memorial. From here, Chinatown and Little Tokyo are easily reached for a good meal.

Walk 2

EL SERENO
Not Even the Natives Know About This

Boundaries: Huntington Dr., Eastern Ave., Alhambra Ave., Winchester Ave.
Rating: 2 Oranges, 1 Peach

Notes From My Journal:
Just what is it that I appreciate about L.A.? I love the variety and the vitality, the opportunities it has afforded immigrants over a period of time to establish themselves in a comfortable life, the vegetation that has color and demands little care and the neighborhoods that have been here for a long time but are hardly known by those living in some other part of L.A.

■ El Sereno is such a neighborhood. It is predominantly Chicano. Surrounded by arterial streets such as Valley Drive, Soto, Eastern and Druid, and 4-5 miles from downtown L.A., it has surprisingly much open space The circling hills, sparsely covered with grasses, project the memory of cattle and horses grazing. I relish the contrast of a nonurban atmosphere so close to a dynamic city center. That, in conjunction with development of the ridges for home and apartment sites and renovation of some areas of decay, is El Sereno history in process.

■ We begin our walk at Chadwick Drive (2900 N.) between Lynnfield St. and Chester St. Immediately we have a great view of the hills to the north, and a question: why are five steps built on this little peninsula of a street which leads up to a private residence?

■ Facing Chadwick Circle, we walk around it toward our right (2700.) Most of the homes here are small, well-kept, single-family residences. Hills are all around us, but it doesn't seem impossible to build on them. The air is good, and the residents we talk to say there is always a breeze, which they appreciate. We hear the children's voices at the school below.

■ Across from 2809 Chadwick Circle is Far Place stairway, which we descend. It's a long stairway; a young girl walking up with her skateboard counts 124 steps. An intersection, Lynnfield Circle, divides the upper from the lower stairway. We continue down, and then turn left on Ballard. The small houses are owner-occupied, generally in good condition, and a source of stability in the community. The yards have abundant flowers and cacti. Turn right on Chester (5000 E.) and walk to Round Drive. Turn right on Round Drive (2800 N.) and continue to Newark. Now we walk on unpaved footpaths, and the views are great.

■ This area is in the process of further home development. As each circle becomes filled with residences, stairways end at the bottom of a slope in someone's backyard. El Sereno is one of the last areas of the city with desirable lots for sale.

■ Turn right on Newark (5200 E.) for a short distance. This is the steepest part of the walk. Now turn right on Adkins (no sign) to Chester St. (5000 E.) On our last scouting walk, we found the open field here used as a dump for old refrigerators. Turn left on Chester St. (5000 E.), then turn left on Budau Ave. At the intersection of Far Place and Budau is a sidewalk signature: *J&P Cristich 1926*. Continue on Budau. At the intersection of Phelps Ave. (2700 N.) and Lombardy Blvd. (2600 N.), cross the street. Turn left on Lombardy, passing the intersection of Lombardy Blvd. (2500 N), Ladd Ave. (5100 E.) and Mallory (2500 E.), and walk to Kimball St.

■ Turn right on Kimball St. (5100 E.) As we walk uphill a kestrel flies over our heads, and we see three radio towers and houses on stilts. Kimball becomes a dirt path, so we reverse our direction. The fire department monitors the hillside lots, and we see their posted signs (from May to August) giving the date the lot was last cleared of weeds and debris. Neglected lots are cited, and owners fined. Kimball St. offers great views of the hills to the west and north. We walk by an unusual tree with palmate leaves and spikes sticking out from the trunk, which we think is a *Chorisia insignas*, commonly known as floss silk.

■ Turn left on Lombardy. Continue to the junction with Eastern Ave. Turn right on Eastern, which is the main commercial street of the neighborhood.

■ Turn left on Twining. The section between Mino Court and Grey Dr. is a dirt footpath. Turn left on Betty Dr. Around the corner is a house on a lot covered by green shag rugs, a humorous substitute for grass and a prize water-saving device. Continue past Zane St.

■ Turn left on Kenneth Dr., then bear left on Bowman Blvd. A beautiful specimen of oleander is here and the homes in this section show very good care. Here is another sidewalk signature: *Will F. Peck, contractor, 1925.* As we walk east, Bowman turns into Gambier. At Eastern Ave. we are startled by the glowing red color of the Farmdale Public School on the grounds of the El Sereno Junior High School. On the school walls are pictures of books, also painted red. Continue to Phelps, and turn right on Phelps to walk up the stairway next to 2840 to Lynnfield. Another 97 paces take us to Chadwick Circle (next to 2746.) We thought someone should have one, and now we've found it—a private funicular at 2755 Chadwick!

■ Now veer to the right toward our beginning. We see the four jacaranda trees on the Chadwick "peninsula." They are in full bloom (it is May), and the sight of masses of pink blossoms is one of the bonuses at the end of our walk.

■ This is a long walk, but we register a panorama of homes, hills, and valley, all within the confines of a single neighborhood, El Sereno.

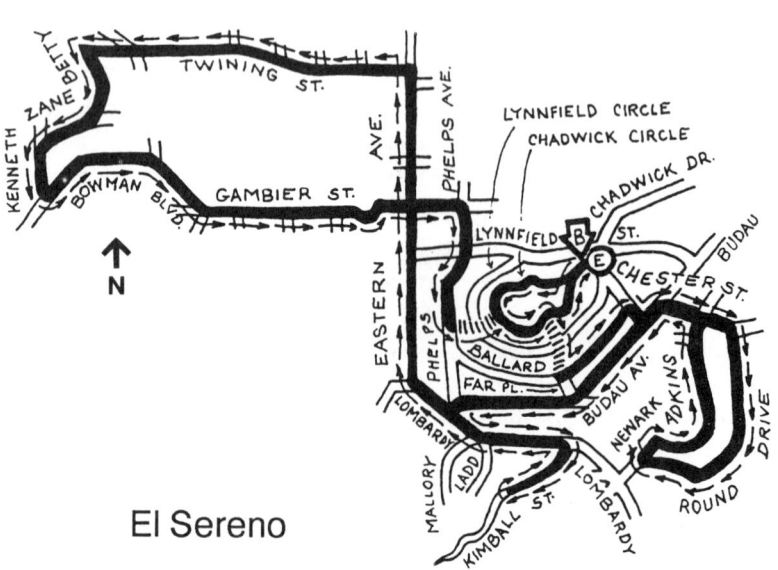

El Sereno

Walk 3

HIGHLAND PARK
Avenue, Lane, Street, Place and Drive

Boundaries: York Blvd., Figueroa St., Pasadena Fwy, Ave. 61, Ave. 66
Rating: 2 Oranges, 1 Tangelo

■ Charles Fletcher Lummis, Highland Park's most noted resident, arrived in December 1885 by foot, from Cincinnati, Ohio. He financed his walk by writing reports for the *L.A. Times*. Subsequently, he was city editor for two years; then magazine editor for *Southwest Land Of Sunshine* (later renamed *Out West*).

■ During his walk to L.A. Charles Lummis was deeply affected by the color, the space and the drama of the landscape. He became convinced of the infinite possibilities of southern California and the Southwest, and dedicated the rest of his life to promoting the area, its arts and architecture, and the rights of Native Americans.

■ Lummis, together with like-minded friends, organized the Sequoya League in 1901 to seek the goal of fair treatment of Indians through legislation. Congressional money to acquire land for displaced Native Americans was one of the results of their work. To further advance the case for the West, Lummis became a sensitive photographer of the Southwest Indians and the desert landscape; he hand-built his house, El Alisal, of native stone; he established the Southwest Museum, which has the finest collection of Southwest Indian arts in the United States.

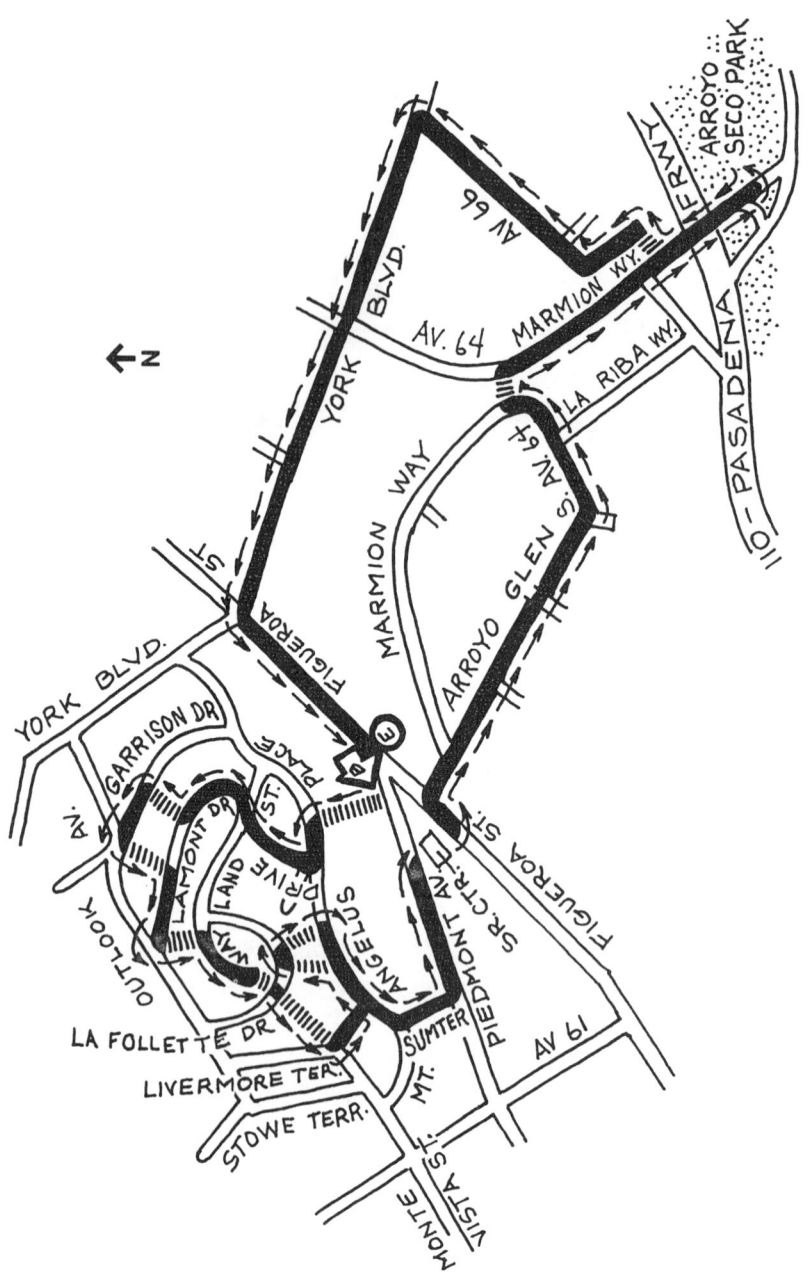

Highland Park

■ The Southwest Museum and El Alisal are the heart of the unusual collection of cultural institutions in the Highland Park neighborhood. In addition there are Heritage Square, an open-air museum of rescued and preserved original buildings from 1865-1920; Casa de Adobe, replica of a 19th century hacienda; and Occidental College.

■ In anticipation of the L.A.-San Gabriel passenger railway, serious home building in the area began in the late 1880s, and within a few years Highland Park became the first area to be annexed to original L.A.

■ The area of Highland Park near Mount Angelus and Ave. 61 has a marked Latino atmosphere, but more Asians and Anglos are moving into the neighborhood, probably displacing the Latinos. Figueroa St., formerly a thriving business section, has suffered a setback since Ivers, a large department store, moved. While the merchants are trying alternative ways to attract new customers, the Highland Park Heritage Trust is actively encouraging appreciation of Highland Park history through house tours and walking tours and preservation of vintage photographs and old buildings. Currently 51 structures in the neighborhood have historic and cultural monument status.

■ The Highland Park neighborhood impressed me with its short streets, but actually these are just streets that end with a stairway or an unpaved section or a house or nothing. Many street names continue for long distances over several segments. However, the generic names—lane, walk and place—change abruptly and constantly. I like that kind of surprise, which throws me slightly off balance and keeps me alert.

■ Begin by ascending the stairway at the cross signs of Figueroa St. (6100 N.) Piedmont Ave. and Mt. Angelus Walk (100 N.) The Highland Park Adult Center is across the street. Gates were installed at the entrance of the Mt. Angelus Walk stairway and some other stairways to prevent thefts and break-ins. If the gate is locked, follow the alternate beginning route given at the end of this walk. Today the gate is open. We pass small houses and gardens that line both sides of the stairway, and at the top, at the intersection of Mt. Angelus Place (6200 E.) and Mt. Angelus Dr. (6200 E.), we see a flowering jacaranda tree.

■ Turn right on Mt. Angelus Dr., walking uphill. Enter Lamont Dr. (200 W.), which bears left. Descend a stairway near 251 Lamont Dr. to Garrison. A magnificent cedar tree stands in front of us.

■ Look out on York Blvd. and see the former police station, dating back to the 1920s. It has been used as a site for movies, and there is a proposal to convert it to a police museum or a community center.

Grimke Stairway

■ Turn left on Garrison to Emerson Walk stairway. Ascend to Lamont Dr. (across from 263). Turn right on Lamont and continue to the charming Grimke stairway. Ascend to 242 Wayland. Echium, roses and jade are planted here. Turn right on Wayland to Monte Vista stairway. Descend to La Follette Dr. (The day we walked, the gate here was locked so we continued right, descending the hill on La Follette Dr. to Outlook Ave. Turn left and continue to Livermore Terr. Turn left and proceed to Monte Vista, where you rejoin the route, which has come down from La Follette on steps.)

■ Continue downward to Mt. Angelus Dr. (6100 E.) Turn left. At 6155 we ascend the stairway to 268 La Follette Dr. Turn right on the stairway (across from 252 La Follette) descending to Mt. Angelus Dr. Go right, then turn left on Sumter Dr. Cross Piedmont Ave. to the Senior Center. (We went in to find out what kinds of activities are available, to talk with some of the people, and to read the bulletin boards, where we found many listings of inviting travel opportunities.)

■ After exiting the center, turn left on Figueroa St.; turn right on Arroyo Glen. 6211 is The Abbey San Encino built around 1915 by Clyde Browne, master printer. The arroyo stone house/castle, set in an acreage of trees, shrubs and cactus is imposing in its appearance of perpetuity. The beautiful round window in the Abbey was designed by the Judson Glass Design Studios, an integral part of the cultural Highland Park community.

Notes From My Journal:
A resident who has lived all her life in the Highland Park neighborhood remembers that Browne, who allowed children to walk through his property, would put out scrap paper from his printing shop for them. (I recall Oscar Wilde's Story "The Selfish Giant" who lived in a state of grace when he allowed children passage through his garden.) She also remembers that Browne permitted children the use of the Abbey basement for Halloween. It was the perfect setting for a Halloween fright because of the shadows and the sounds of the shop machinery. The kids acted scared and screamed. The Abbey, now a private residence, is on the Cultural Heritage list.

■ Turn left on S. Ave. 64, which has nice bungalows on both sides. At the intersection of Marmion Way, ascend the stairway and turn right. (Marmion was part of the old Camino Real connecting the Highland neighborhood with Pasadena. The Red Line electric railway also ran on it.) Cross the Ave 64 Bridge over Freeway 110 into Arroyo Seco Park. Find a bench under the buckeye tree to sit and eat oranges and tangelos.

Notes from My Journal:
The wet arroyo is recalled by a resident as the perfect place for pollywog hunting among the oaks and sycamores, before the Works Progress Administration put in the storm drains during the late 1930s and the Arroyo Seco Parkway was built.

■ Return across the Ave. 64 bridge and ascend the stairway connecting to Ave. 66. Continue northeast on Ave.66. The Judson Glass Design Studios (200 S. Ave. 66), built in 1901 and known as the "Tiffany of the West," still continues the tradition of fine glass work. The Arroyo Guild of Craftsmen met here; their motto, "We Can," is above the entrance.

■ Turn left on York Blvd (6600 E.) Pass the Evangelical Formosan Church at 6501 E. York Blvd. Turn left on Figueroa to Piedmont and our beginning.

■ Route in case the Mt. Angelus Walk stairway is locked: Piedmont to Sumter to Mt. Angelus Dr. to Monte Vista St. E. to Livermore Terr. Ascend the Monte Vista Walk stairway to La Follette to Wayland.

Tour Information:
■ **El Alisal:** Wednesday-Sunday 1-4 P.M. 200 S. Ave 43.
Tel: 222-0546
■ **Heritage Square:** First and second Sunday of Month 11-3 P.M.
3800 Homer St. Tel: 222-3150
■ **Southwest Museum:** Tuesday-Sunday 1-5 P.M. 234 Museum Dr.
Tel: 221-2163
■ **Casa de Adobe:** Wednesday, Saturday, Sunday 1-5 P.M.
4605 N. Figueroa St. Tel: 225-8653

Walk 4

MOUNT WASHINGTON EAST and WEST
An Articulated Walk

Boundaries: Mt. Washington Dr., Ave. 50, San Rafael Ave., Marmion Way
Rating: (see separate sections)

■ Mt. Washington, about 1600 feet high, is located in the northeast part of L.A. The surrounding neighborhood is one of our very favorite areas. The beauty here evokes a feeling of tranquility and, as we round a bend, surprise at seeing an extension of a view that we had not imagined. It is similar to experiencing, in piecemeal form, a panoramic photograph.

■ Downtown is 10^+ physical minutes away; the psychological distance is thousands of minutes. We see hawks circling in the air, squirrels scampering up the eucalyptus, imaginatively designed homes, home-brewed "architecture without architects," luxuriant vegetation and expansive views of the San Gabriel Mountains, Verdugo Hills, San Rafael Hills, Lincoln Heights Valley and downtown L.A. Through it all, we feel nestled in and charmed. It is easy to understand the affection Jack Smith of the *L.A. Times* and a resident of Mt. Washington expresses for the neighborhood through his columns. It is also easy to see why so many of the locals of the area settle in for several generations.

■ This walk is separated into two parts to encompass the contrasting attractions in Mt. Washington. The eastern half, around Marmion Way

22   *Stairway Walks in Los Angeles*

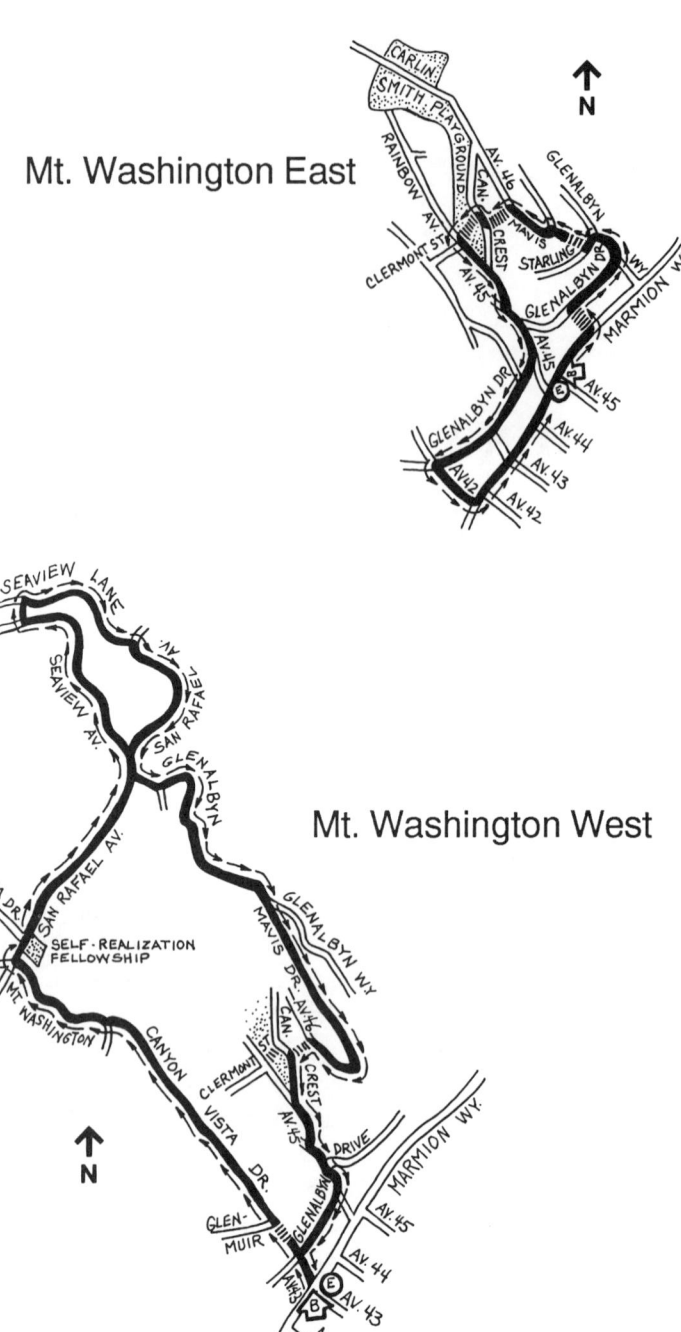

and Ave. 45, has many changes in elevation that give us different perspectives on what we see. The western half, around San Rafael Ave. and Elyria, has more plateaus from which we see broad views.

MT. WASHINGTON EAST

Rating: 3 Oranges

■ We begin our walk at Marmion Way and Ave. 45. Walk a few yards north and to the right of the garage of 4547. Ascend a stairway with a long intermediate footpath. Wooden homes that date back to the beginning of the century are on either side of the pathway. The lots are large and irregular.

■ We continue uphill to our right on Glenalbyn Dr. On the right-hand side of 4591 is a tree house in a eucalyptus. 4648, a Moderne, and 4652 are built on lots that seem just short of vertical. Turn left on Starling Way (4500 N.) Pepper trees, acacias and pines are all around. We sight the Southwest Museum on the right-hand side, and today we see Pasadena toward the east.

Notes From My Journal:
The mountain peak above Pasadena was named for Benjamin D. Wilson (Don Benito), who came to California in the 1830s. He became a ranchero, a highly respected agriculturist and the first mayor of L.A.

■ Next to 4567 Starling Way we ascend the stairway made of cement and railroad ties. Continue on the dirt walkway, which is partially canopied by the branches of the old trees. On our left is a corrugated aluminum fence enclosing a house with a window wall. Follow the railroad ties toward the right.

■ A hard turn right, in front of a large jade plant, reveals the wooden stairway (right of 340) that we ascend. At the top of the stairway, turn left on Mavis Dr.

Notes From My Journal:
Everybody gets lost around here. Don't feel bad. We met a man from a security service who was trying to find the house where he expected to make a call. A resident tells us that she gives directions to many truck drivers who have consulted their Thomas Bros. maps, but still find themselves lost and disoriented by the stairways.

24 *Stairway Walks in Los Angeles*

Clermont Stairway

MT. WASHINGTON EAST

■ The structures are handsome and varied and there is much activity with new construction and additional upgrading of homes. The yards are lovely, but Mavis Dr. still has cracks and holes.

■ Continue just beyond the house on Mavis Dr. (300 W.) to descend the Clermont stairway, beginning at the intersection of Ave. 46 (400 W.) and Clermont St. (4500 N.) The risers are just the perfect height to make the descent to Canyon Crest easy. This is a delightful woodsy area with lots of foliage color. To our left is a super-size thatch tree house. At the bottom of Clermont St. stairway (4500 N.) we turn right, crossing Canyon Crest Dr., and almost immediately turn left to descend the remaining section of the stairway to the picnic area in Carlin Smith playground. Cross the picnic area to Ave. 45, which is called Rainbow Ave., to our right.

■ Turn left to the junction of Clermont (4400 W.) and Ave. 45 (300 W.) and walk down the Ave. 45 hill past the sign saying "Ave. 45 (300 W.)" To our right are cottages from the 1930s; however, 335 was built in 1978.

■ Continue walking one-half block past the street sign on the left, Glenalbyn Dr. (4500 N.) to the street sign on our right, Glenalbyn Dr. (4400 N.) Turn right.

■ 4344 is a Victorian with a pitched roof, fish-scale and battan siding and a comical dunce cap. 4225 is a wood shingle house with fieldstone chimney, porch and retaining wall. It has a vaguely Midwest feeling. Vegetation is varied and abundant. 4211 Glenalbyn appears only to be a four-car brick-facing garage. However, when we look upward we see built above it a charming, weathered, ivy-covered pergola with slatted sides, complimented by ornamental metal-and-glass light standards. We can only imagine the attractive hidden residence.

■ Left turn at the corner of Ave. 42 (300 W.) and Glenalbyn. 219 Ave. 42 is a large Craftsman-style house, a style we find conducive to comfortable living. Walk down to Marmion and turn left to our beginning at Ave. 45.

Notes From My Journal:
One day I will design a walk tracing the ubiquitous Glenalbyns—place, way, drive!

MT. WASHINGTON WEST
Trek to the Self-Realization Fellowship on 3880 San Rafael Ave. And Beyond

Rating: 2 Oranges, $1/2$ Cantaloupe

■ Mt. Washington Dr. along the arroyo was the old carriage route to the summit. Accessible transportation via the L.A. & Santa Fe railroad opened the Mt. Washington area in 1884, and the first houses were built on the hill in 1907. In 1909 the L.A. & Mt. Washington incline railway operated a 2-car cable rail that paralleled the present Canyon Vista Dr. The destination was the luxurious and popular trysting place, Mt. Washington Hotel, at 3880 San Rafael Ave. During the 1920s hunting lodges were built at the top. Now the lodges are gone and the railways are defunct. The hotel reopened in 1925 as the international headquarters of the Self-Realization Fellowship, founded by Paramahansa Yogananda.

■ We begin at Ave. 43 and Marmion Way. Walk up the Ave. 43 hill and ascend the angled concrete stairway near the intersection of Glenmuir. Continue westward on Canyon Vista Dr. toward the intersection of Mt. Washington Dr. Bear right on Mt. Washington Dr. to San Rafael Ave. Turn right on San Rafael Ave. Turn right on Elyria Dr. into the grounds of the Fellowship.

■ There are 10 acres of grounds, and the plantings feature fine specimens of a variety of trees—coral, camphor, and tupidanthus. Luther Burbank, the horticulturalist and plant breeder (1849-1926), gave the swami a spineless cactus which is still thriving. A white gazebo for meditation and a wishing well for spiritual wishes are two structures along the pedestrian path.

■ The main building is open to visitors, and has a lounge with very comfortable seating and a library of books relating to the fellowship. A receptionist at the desk answers questions and arranges short informal tours.

■ When we go out the main gate of the Fellowship, we turn right on San Rafael and shortly pass the Mt. Washington School (the children are enjoying life in the playground—no school today). Veer to the left on Seaview *Avenue* to connect with Seaview *Lane*.

■ Turn right on Seaview Lane. The extraordinary view of the surrounding hills and mountains makes us feel expansive and eager to continue walking. Most of the homes here are custom-designed, and there are striking examples of contemporary architecture. 4226 and 4234 are noteworthy. At 4163 is an example of Craftsman style. Situated back from the street, it has a rear balcony instead of a front porch for greater privacy.

■ At the juncture of Seaview *Lane* and San Rafael, turn right on San Rafael; then turn left on Glenalbyn, and veer right on Mavis Dr., which curves right until we reach Ave. 46 (400 W.) At that point, Mavis becomes Ave. 46. Walk to the left and descend the Clermont stairway, beginning at the intersection of Clermont St. (4500 N.), Mavis Dr. (300 W.) and Ave. 46 (400 W.) to Canyon Crest.

■ Turn left on Canyon Crest to Ave. 45. Then turn left on Ave. 45 to Glenalbyn. Turn right for one block to Ave. 43. Turn left and go downhill to Marmion Way, where we see the desert tan structure at 202 Ave. 43, formerly the 1909 cable-car station, now a private residence.

Shorter Return Route from the Fellowship Headquarters

■ Turn left, south, on San Rafael Ave. from the gate. Turn left on Mt. Washington Dr. and bear left onto Canyon Vista Dr. Descend the Glenmuir stairway, and continue down to Glenalbyn, Ave. 43 and Marmion Way.

Notes From My Journal:
In 1907 Robert Marsh and Co, laid out the streets of Mt. Washington, including the crown of the hill, all part of Rancho San Rafael.

Walks 5 and 6
Introduction

Although the Echo Park and Elysian Heights area is just north of the downtown skyscrapers, very little has changed from the look of 50 years ago. And that is rare in a city just now falling out of love with the philosophy of "rip 'em down and build something new." To be sure, Echo Park's population has changed; it is now home to many working-class Latino and Asian families, many of them recent immigrants, mixed in with old Anglo residents, aging hippies and a new influx of professionals looking for decent housing close to downtown. There are some slums, and problems with graffiti and gangs.

Still, this hillside community is a comfortable place with a real sense of history, a mixture of inner-city and country-lane living. Its many houses from the Thirties, Twenties and even, in some cases, the 1880's are cherished for their character and their spacious yards. Its shopping district on Sunset Blvd. is a lively, ethnic potpourri and its hilltops offer stunning views. Dodger Stadium is an easy walk away, and the neighborhood is blessed with two famous parks: Echo Park itself, with its lake and geyser fountain; and Elysian Park, whose 600 acres make it the second largest park in L.A., after Griffith Park.

Walk 5

ECHO PARK
Gingerbread Houses and Sports Stars

Boundaries: Glendale Blvd., the Hollywood Freeway, Sunset Blvd.
Rating: 2 Oranges

■ We start in front of the Angelus Temple, at the intersection of Glendale Blvd. 1000 N. and Park Ave., at the northern end of Echo Park lake, just across from the California Federal bank highrise. The temple was built in 1925 as the headquarters of evangelist Aimee Semple McPherson. Designed to resemble the Mormon Tabernacle in Salt Lake City, the domed structure is still home to McPherson's Four Square Gospel Church and is very busy on Sundays and holidays. We cross Park and walk on the footpath along the western side of the lake, bordering Glendale Blvd. Echo Park lake itself is one of L.A.'s most photographed sites and has been used as a setting for many movies. Taking up most of the park's 26 acres, the lake has some enormous lotus plants, an attractive wooden footbridge and an armada of rental paddleboats. Its best feature, however, is the geyser fountain in its center, which was happily refurbished in time for the 1984 Olympics. Its enormous spray sends a message of coolness even to the harried commuters on the nearby Hollywood Freeway.

■ Halfway down the lake, after signs for Santa Ynez and Kent Sts., we will be across from the twin-sided Clinton St. stairway, covered with a mural showing athletes in motion. At the crosswalk, we carefully cross busy Glendale Blvd. to the west side. The mural was another gift from the

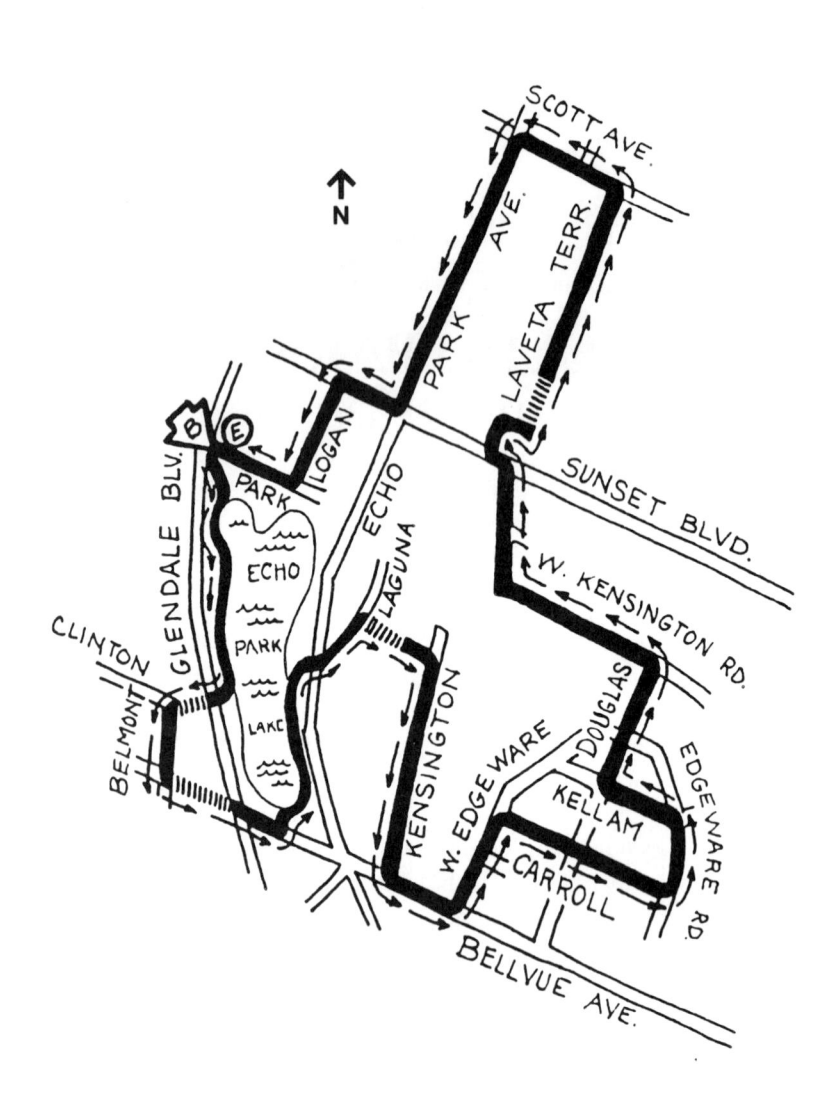

Echo Park

1984 Olympic era. It is sometimes scarred by graffiti, but that does not dim its powerfully painted images of runners, swimmers, bikers and baseball players. We ascend the stairway and at its top will be Belmont Ave. Turn left on Belmont, and in one block is a concrete stairway at Bellevue Ave., just next to the splendid California bungalow at #508 Belmont. We descend that zig-zag Belmont stairway back down to Glendale Blvd. and cross Glendale at the light back to the southern end of the park. We stroll along the bottom of the lake along Bellevue Ave. and turn left up the footpath on its eastern side which runs parallel to Echo Park Ave. About halfway up the lake, we cross over to the built-up side of the street. There are great examples of hillside, courtyard bungalows at #650-684 Echo Park Ave. with their private stairway in the center. This is a very Mediterranean-looking spot, which conjures thoughts of Echo Park as the setting of Raymond Chandler novels. We veer right onto Laguna Ave. by St. Athanasius Episcopal Church on the corner. This wood shingled church, built in 1890, seems lost from the English Countryside but has a vibrant parish with many community outreach programs, including a well-known organization which works to keep youngsters out of gangs. The building itself, however, may be doomed, as the Episcopal archdiocese is planning its headquarters and a new church on the site.

■ Along Laguna, we will pass homes built on hills with steep stairs to their front doors. We can stop to notice the rounded, brick stairs at #844 Laguna and just after that comes a row of garages and then a public stairway, the Crosby Place steps which we climb. Sometimes cluttered with refuse, these steps are bordered by old palm trees and offer great views of the lake. On top, we walk straight ahead for a block and turn right on Kensington which goes downhill and turn left on Bellevue Ave.

■ At the second corner, turn left on W. Edgeware Rd. We are now in the architectural preservation district called Angelino Heights, one of the few areas in the city where all architectural changes must be in keeping with the original spirit, in this case Victoriana of the 1880s and turn-of-the-century Craftsman style. Some are rundown, although visible evidence of what was once a very fashionable area. But there is a growing restoration movement, particularly along Carroll and Kellam Avenues, and the restorationists are adding political activism and street festivals to the scene.

■ We turn right on Carroll for a real treat, the splendid Queen Anne and Gingerbread houses that make you forget you are in a new, tropical city.

Laveta Stairway

Two houses, #1343 and #1325, were even moved from other neighborhoods onto the block recently to aid in the revival. Particularly note: #1345 Carroll, with its wrought iron railings on its widow's walk; #1330 and its second-story porch; the tower at #1320. Wander on Carroll, past Douglas St., eventually making a left turn onto the other end of the circular Edgeware Rd. and a left turn again on Kellam Ave., which has its own share of charming houses. Turn right on Douglas St. and in two blocks turn left on W. Kensington Rd. The restored Victorian at #892 Kensington and the big Craftsman style at #902 are interesting. Turn right at Laveta Terrace and we follow it down the hill to Sunset Blvd. We cross Sunset at the light and turn left. At the corner, Laveta picks up again and we turn right onto it. We follow Laveta around the bend; very soon, on our left, just across from 1322 Laveta, is what was once one of the most elegant stairways in the city. Now poorly maintained, the wide Laveta stairs are reminiscent of Italian piazza steps and have overhanging-lips, broad side-arms and gracious lampposts. Residents complained that an overzealous Hollywood director recently filmed an auto chase scene there, badly cracking some of the steps; barrier poles now stop any accidental or purposeful car rides down the steps.

■ We ascend and walk straight ahead on Laveta, watching the proud, symmetrical line of very tall Royal palm trees. Turn left on Scott Ave. and in two blocks cross Echo Park Ave. and turn left along it. Continue on Echo Park Ave. At #1325 is a branch of the famous Phoenix bakery, whose headquarters are in Chinatown. Here we can sample Chinese takeout and some of the best baked goodies in town, especially the cream and strawberry birthday cakes. Next door, for fast food fanatics, is the original stand of Pioneer Chicken. On the other side of the street is a lively newsstand which offers newspapers and magazines from many different Latin American countries to immigrants hungry for word of home. This area is also known for home-style, ethnic restaurants, such as Barragan's Mexican eatery at #1538 Sunset. We cross Sunset and turn left on its other side.

■ Because of its proximity to Dodger Stadium, this stretch of Sunset was dubbed Avenue of the Athletes and its sidewalks are sporadically dotted with plaques honoring famous sportsmen and sportswomen who have California connections. However, the plaques can be hard to find by passersby and the street is no rival for the star-studded sidewalks of Hollywood Blvd. So keep your eyes peeled to the sidewalk on our side of Sunset, in front of the clothes store at #1606 Sunset for the plaque for track star Parry O'Brien. Between the tavern at #1616 and the clothes shop at #1618 is one for tennis player Jack Kramer. In front of the Two Dollar Bill's store at #1624 are Olympian trackman Bob Seagren and baseball great Sandy Koufax. (On the other side of Sunset, along the wall for the Pioneer Market parking lot are the plaques for baseball's Jackie Robinson, basketball's Bill Sharman, Dodger manager Tommy Lasorda, and Ellsworth Vines of tennis. Everyone but fanatics can probably skip seeing those because of the heavy traffic near the market.) Continuing on our side of Sunset, near the corner of Logan is a plaque for a non-athlete: it honors L. Andrew Castle, the late owner of the camera store at the end of the block; his plaque's symbol is a camera.

■ We turn left on Logan and follow it to Park. We turn right and we are back at the lake and Angelus Temple.

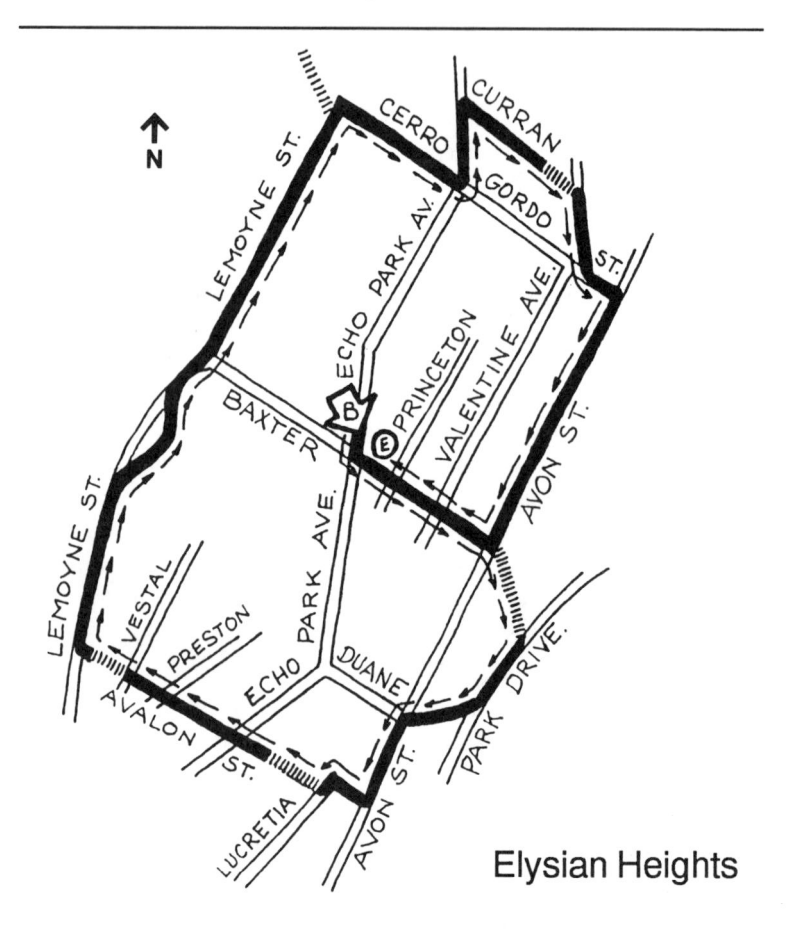

Elysian Heights

Walk 6

ELYSIAN HEIGHTS
Memorial to a Cat Named Room 8

Boundaries: Glendale Blvd., the Glendale Freeway, Scott Ave., Stadium Way
Rating: 3 Oranges

■ We start at the Elysian Heights Elementary School, located at the intersection of Echo Park Ave. and Baxter St., at #1562 Baxter. Along the Echo Park Ave. side is a remarkable and delightful memorial—or group of memorials—to the late and lamented school mascot. Yes, a cat. In the concrete sidewalk along the fence are about 30 written or drawn tributes to the kitty who came one day in 1952 to schoolyard, was adopted by the class in Room 8 and stayed for the next 16 years. Appropriately, he was named Room 8. One sample:

> "Without a Name
> To Room 8 He Came
> To Give Our School
> The Greatest Fame."

■ Not on display is the book two teachers wrote about Room 8. But, we should not miss the painted mural of Room 8 along that side of the school.
■ Heading back toward Baxter, we turn left on that street and walk in front of the school's main entrance. We continue up Baxter, past Princeton and Valentine Sts. At the next intersection, the one with Avon St. 2100,

the enormous Baxter Street stairway will be just over our right shoulder, about a quarter block ahead up Baxter.

■ We start to climb the breathtakingly steep stairway as it zigzags up. Ascending, we walk past the grassy hillside, spotted with jade and iceplant. This concrete stairway is in excellent condition and hikers can take a break and sit on one of its steps to contemplate the fine views of the Hollywood sign and Griffith Observatory.

■ On top, follow the gravel path, which merges with a private driveway, to the street directly ahead. Turn right on that street, which is Park Drive. We are on a high ridge bordering Elysian Park. The park and its thousands of Eucalyptus trees are on our left side, along with a hint of Dodger Stadium and its vast parking lots; Silver Lake and Griffith Park on the right; the downtown skyscrapers and Art Deco City Hall tower are straight ahead. Yet, this remains secluded and is beloved for its private, nearly rural flavor. Walking here can cause a feeling of dislocation: are we in the country or the city?

■ We turn right at Duane St., where it intersects with Park Dr. 1900 N. Down in the hollow over our right shoulders, we can see the Elysian Heights Elementary School. Duane St. curves directly into Avon St. At the first intersection, which is with Morton Ave. 1800 and Lucretia Ave. 1800N., we turn right onto Lucretia. In that first block of Lucretia, just after it curves is the entrance to the wooden Avalon St. stairway. It is located on the right side of the street, between #1895 and #1889 Lucretia. We descend. The Avalon stairway was damaged in a fire in 1985 and still shows some scars under the white paint but city engineers insist it is safe. The climb down its 170 steps and boardwalk bridges can be a bit scary after all that solid concrete but the effort is worthwhile. Again, the views of Hollywood are great.

■ At the bottom, we continue on Avalon St. and cross Echo Park Ave. Continuing on Avalon, we pass Preston Ave. and then at the intersection with Vestal Ave. 1900 N. is a concrete stairway. We ascend that second Avalon St. stairway and can pause to see the sweet bungalows along the stairs and the well-tended yucca and jade plants. The gate at #1810 looks like an English coachhouse and the garden in front seems like an oasis from city life.

■ On top, we turn right onto what is Lemoyne St. 1800N. and follow Lemoyne for the equivalent of about four blocks. In front of the English-style house at #2005, Lemoyne is split by a center island. We take the upper portion on our right and continue on Lemoyne past Baxter, noticing the wooden, modern townhouses at #2106. Finally, Lemoyne ends at Cerro Gordo St. 1800.

■ At that intersection is a city-owned water tank and just to the left of that tank is a small concrete stairway. There is no sign but it is called Wiles Pl. For a brief but astonishing detour, we climb up those stairs and follow the brick path and then wooden stairs to a hillside enclave of homes, secluded to the extreme. The wooden house at #2312 looks like a Russian dacha. The public walkway really ends there, so we must resist the temptation to continue. We turn around and walk back to the water tower, descend the stairway and turn left on Cerro Gordo.

■ In two blocks, Cerro Gordo intersects with Echo Park Ave. We turn left on Echo Park and turn right at the next street, which is Curran St. We continue on Curran for one block until it ends at the top of the Curran St. stairway. We descend this well-maintained stairway and only the sight of the freeway in the distance spoils the country atmosphere for the homes along the steps. Turn right at the bottom, which is Valentine St.

■ Turn left at the first corner, which is the intersection of Valentine and Cerro Gordo 1500 N. We walk on Cerro Gordo for a block and turn right onto Avon St. We follow Avon St., past the two entrances to circular Avon Park Terrace and Donaldson St, and come to the intersection with Baxter St. Over our left shoulders will be the Baxter St. stairway that we climbed earlier. We turn right on Baxter, going away from the stairway, and return to the Elysian Heights school.

Walks 7 and 8
Introduction

Silver Lake belies the notion that Los Angeles is just a soul-less blur of commercial strips and housing tracts. Huddled around a gorgeous reservoir, this hillside neighborhood is a lively mixture of Anglo, Latino, Asian, gay and straight residents, of street life and privacy. Its hillside homes, and many stairways, offer wonderful views of downtown skyscrapers and of nearby mountain ranges. Its shopping streets offer a funky mixture of avante-garde cafes and old-fashioned services missing from the trendier, and more expensive, regions of the city's better known Westside. The mixture of nature and city (only ten minutes from downtown) has long attracted artists and designers to Silver Lake and the area is dotted with the work of such famous architects as Richard Neutra and R.M. Schindler.

For stairway walkers, Silver Lake can at times have the feel of a Mediterranean village, especially when the blue water of its namesake reservoir, built in 1900 and the oldest in the city, peeks through. We have divided up the area into two walks—on the eastern and on the western side of the reservoir. As one of the oldest and hilliest neighborhoods in the city, Silver Lake has many—more than 40—stairways, some of which do not fit easily into a roundtrip walk. So, if you have time, visit some of its other stairways listed in our index.

Walk 7

SOUTHWEST SILVER LAKE
Above the Blue Water with Laurel and Hardy

Boundaries: Silverlake Blvd., Sunset Blvd., W. Silverlake Dr.
Rating: 3 Oranges

■ We begin our walk at what is probably the most famous urban stairway in America: the ones up which Stan Laurel and Oliver Hardy hilariously tried to carry a piano in their Academy Award winning film of 1932, "The Music Box." This concrete stairway is located between #921 and #935 Vendome St., just off of Sunset Blvd., near the cross street of Del Monte Dr. 3300. Film historians tried, without success, to have it declared a city landmark and it still attracts its share of visitors. The stairway was recently renovated and given modern light fixtures and railings; so its place in movie history is not easily recognizable. But as we ascend it, past the old Spanish style homes and courtyards along the stairs, we can imagine the early days of the Hollywood film industry, which had several of its studios in the Silver Lake area. As the noise of Sunset abates, we approach Descanso Drive on top and turn left on Descanso. We follow along Descanso's island of trees and flowers. Between 3375 and 3365 Descanso is a long, sometimes littered stairway to Sunset. Skip that and continue another block, noticing the spectacular views of downtown's skyscrapers. Turn right on Micheltorena St. At the end of the block, at the intersection with Winslow Dr., is the start of the Micheltorena stairway, one of the grandest stairways in the city. We start to descend the first of its 218 steps

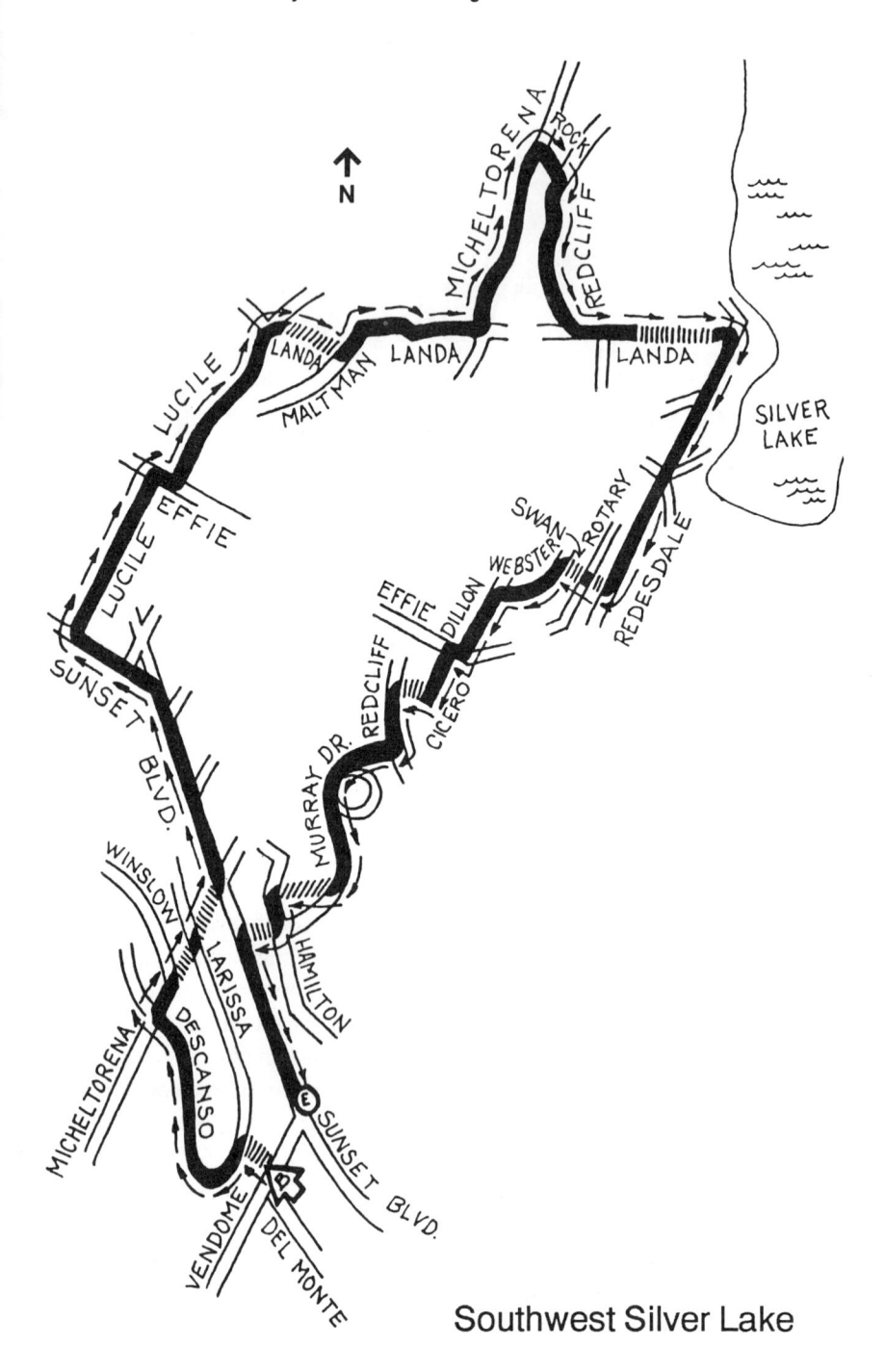

Southwest Silver Lake

and continue, crossing Larissa Dr., down to Sunset Blvd. There are several houses whose only access is off the stairs; particularly interesting are #1361 and #1367 Micheltorena.

■ This stairway bears the scars of city life: graffiti and some refuse. But one nearby resident called it "magical and mystical" even though he complained that it took a fib to get the stairs cleaned up recently. After what he said were many previous telephone calls to the city's street maintenance crews, he said he called once more and made up a tale that the mayor was about to visit the stairway for a ceremony. Within a couple of hours, a crew was cutting back weeds and collecting litter there. Micheltorena Street itself was named after another California official: General Manuel Micheltorena, next to the last of the Mexican governors of California. Micheltorena established a system of public education. However, his term (1842-45) was notorious for the plundering by his rag-tag army. Micheltorena was undone by a revolt which eventually led to American control.

■ On Sunset, turn left and walk four blocks and turn right at Lucile Ave. Cross Sunset and continue up Lucile.

■ (Before heading up Lucile, you may want to explore this interesting shopping area along Sunset, with its boutiques and eateries, its Latin and gay flavors. Among the highlights: El Conquistador, a lovely Mexican restaurant at #3705 Sunset; the Olio, a bohemian theater at #3709; Ozzie Dots used clothes shop at #3906; the Seafood Bay restaurant at #3916, beloved for its very fresh and inexpensive fish; La Perlita bakery at #3918. If you take this detour, come back to Lucile and turn left up the hill from the north side of Sunset.)

■ We take Lucile for two blocks and turn right on Effie St. and a quick left turn on the continuation of Lucile. Bear to the left, staying on Lucile at its intersection with Carnation. At #1830 Lucile is the well known Falk Apartments, R. M. Schindler's 1939 project that seems to combine Bauhaus and Japanese aesthetics. We walk up and down its center staircase and see how he created a hillside village and gave each apartment its own small garden and views of Hollywood. We continue along Lucile another block to Landa St.

■ We turn right and ascend the Landa St. stairway. We pass Edgecliff Dr. and continue up. We can turn around to catch the vistas of Griffith Park, the Griffith Observatory, the Hollywood sign. The three secluded homes along the upper walkway occupy a dream spot with rare quiet. Especially charming is #3616 Landa, an ivy-covered house English-style house. On the other hand, living there has its problems: mailmen and newspaper boys will climb the steps but garbage pickup crews won't; so the residents have to carry in their own groceries and drag their trash to the top or bottom of the stairs. On top, we turn left on Maltman which curves into Landa. We will be passing along the walls on the right hand side of what once was the five-acre estate of silent screen star Antonio Moreno. It is now the Immaculate Conception Home for Girls. The secluded complex was damaged in the October 1987 earthquake.

■ We turn left at the intersection of Landa and Micheltorena. We are now on the spine of a steep, lush hill, lined with expensive homes that have views of the reservoir. The imaginative stucco house at #1856 Micheltorena was designed by Gregory Ain in 1939. At #2109, we make the sharp-angled right turn onto Rock St., which soon will merge into Redcliff St. In another block, turn left onto the much-interrupted Landa St. On Landa, we walk past Castle St. until the stairway at the end of Landa. In the distance, we can see the cross of Forest Lawn Cemetery in Glendale in the hills on the other side of Silver Lake reservoir. We descend the winding stairway, bedecked with wildflowers, jade plants and cacti.

■ At the bottom, turn right along Redesdale Ave. A busy, small park is on the left. Continue on Redesdale (avoid the urge to follow the joggers on West Silverlake Dr. around the park) for another three short blocks and watch for the sign for Swan Pl. Just across from #1760 Redesdale at Swan is a steep and utilitarian stairway which we ascend up to Rotary Dr. and then continue up directly ahead on stairway up to Webster Ave. At the top, we turn left on Webster and catch our breath for a succession of quick turns: turn left on Dillon, turn right on Effie, turn left on Cicero Dr. Between #1637 and #1631 Cicero is a charming stairway; we descend and notice the quaint little house on our left as we go down.

■ At the bottom, we turn left on Redcliff Ave. At the first intersection we turn right on Murray Dr. (avoid Murray Circle). There is an interesting garden at #1536. After #1523 Murray Dr. and the lot next door, and just to the right of #1511, is the concrete Murray stairway. We descend and turn left at the bottom on Hamilton Way.

■ At the intersection of Hamilton 3300W and Murray Dr. 1400N, between #3224 and #3300 Hamilton is another stairway. We descend this stairway, which can be messy at times. That reminds us, as we get closer to Sunset, that Silver Lake is in the midst of the city. At the bottom, we are on Sunset and we turn left. We continue for a block and a half to Vendome and cross Sunset and we are back at our starting point.

Walk 8

EASTERN SILVER LAKE
The Streetcar Doesn't Stop Here Anymore

Boundaries: Silver Lake Blvd., Allesandro St.,Riverside Dr., Fletcher Dr.
Rating: 3 Oranges

■ This walk takes us through a varied landscape of hills, landmark homes, busy streets and country-like quiet. Eastern Silver Lake has been cut off from much of the world by the Golden State and Glendale Freeways; that has given the neighborhood more of a sense of place, ironically, and sometimes a sense of a place happy to be forgotten by the rest of Los Angeles.

■ We begin near the intersection of Silverlake Blvd. 2400 N. and Glendale Blvd. (If heading by car north from downtown along Glendale Blvd., turn left on Silverlake; if heading south on Glendale, turn right. A Bank of America branch and a Chevron station are at the intersection.If heading north on Silverlake, stop just after Earl St. Park on the 2400 block of Silverlake Blvd.)

■ Wealthy homeowners and ambitious architects used this boulevard to work out their house dreams in days when there was much less auto traffic and the reservoir's previous configuration brought the water closer to the road here. As a result, it is dotted with landmarks of the Modernist and International movement, particularly of Richard Neutra. At #2300 Silverlake Blvd. is Neutra's home, originally built in 1933 and partially rebuilt

Earl Stairway

by his son Dion in 1963 after a fire. This house, remarkably advanced for its era, uses glass and roof-top ponds to bring nature into everyday living. His widow has willed it to Cal Poly Pomona architecture school. (The Neutra firm still has an office around the corner on Glendale Blvd.) Continuing along the boulevard is what some call Neutraland: a string of five houses—#2226, 2232, 2238, 2242 and 2250—from the late Forties to through late Fifties. Each is like a piece of Modernist sculpture, horizontal planes of glass and wood. The next intersection is Cove Ave. where we turn left.

■ At the top of the street is the Cove Ave. stairway. This is a wonderful concrete stairway that has stunning views of the water and of Griffith Park. Its shallow and long steps are lined in parts with cedar trees. As we climb to the apex, the feel is like a stroll in an Italian Alpine town. Walk another block across Apex Ave. and turn right for about 50 feet. Just across from #2121 Apex is a set of stairs through an old but well-kept court of wooden bungalows from the 1920's. Lined with ivy and snapdragons, it is a relic of a style of Los Angeles life that is fast disappearing, replaced by highrises and shopping centers. We descend and turn left onto Glendale Blvd. and carefully cross this busy thoroughfare. In two blocks, turn right onto Loma Vista Place. On our right is a quirky, castle-like home at #2384; its mosaic, wavy walls and blue color give it an Alice in Wonderland style and seem to consciously imitate the work of Barcelona's Antonio Gaudi.

■ Straight ahead is the start of what is probably the longest, uninterrupted stairway and walkway in the city. It goes up and down the hill in a series of steps and paths lined with trees and bungalows. (However, beware of loose dogs here; we were made a little wiser by a set of canine teeth ripping through a pair of pants. Happily, neither dog nor walker was hurt and the dog's owner paid for a new pair of pants.) At one point, Loma Vista widens out to a double set of concrete stairs and sidewalk as the adjacent hills of Elysian Park come into view. Palm trees and jade plants abound in a neighborhood that has a taste of Sixties hippiedom still flourishing. Another long stairway brings us down to Allesandro Way and the fencing of the Glendale Freeway. Turn left and make another left turn at the next corner, Earl St. We bear right along Earl and just across from #2261, near a street sign for Bancroft Ave., is the gigantic zigzagging Earl St. steps which we ascend to the top. These, like many in the neighborhood, were built as shortcuts to the old streetcar lines, now mourned by natives as auto-choked Los Angeles starts building an expensive subway.

■ On top, turn right quickly right onto Hidalgo Ave. and follow it for a long stretch, with fine views of the reservoir on your left. After the third intersection, Ayr St., Hidalgo will end in a stairway, spotted with jade and cactus, which we descend. On the Hidalgo Ave. stairway, we can see vistas of Forest Lawn Cemetery in Glendale and of the San Gabriel Mountains. At the bottom, we turn right on Electric St, which we follow until it bends to the right and becomes Silver Ridge Ave. Around the bend, between #2506 and #2494 Silver Ridge is a concrete stairway in between secluded hillside gardens and homes. We descend and turn left at the bottom on Lake View Ave. (Do not take the stairway straight across Lake View.)

■ We turn left at India St. 2500 and walk down the hill to Silver Lake Blvd. where we turn left. Silver Lake Blvd. makes a 90 degree right turn at the next intersection, which is Teviot St. We turn right, staying on Silver Lake and we are back at Glendale Blvd. and our starting point in a block.

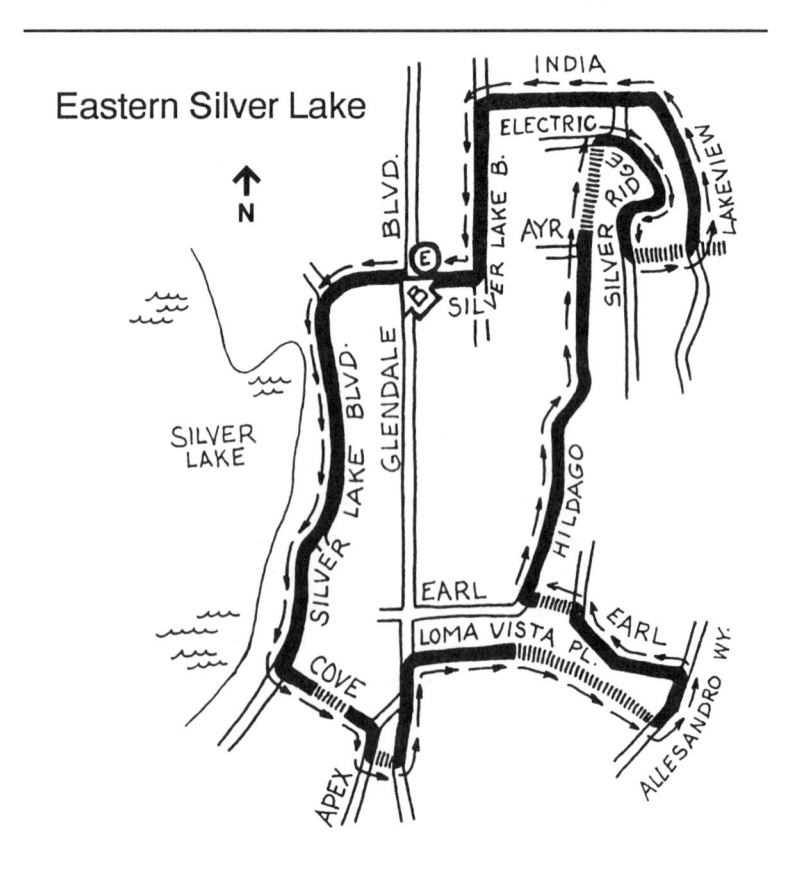

Eastern Silver Lake

Walk 9

FRANKLIN HEIGHTS
Detours, Uphills, and No Sidewalks

Boundaries: Los Feliz Blvd., Hyperion Ave., Fountain Ave., Vermont St.
Rating: 2 Oranges, 3 Raisins

■ Franklin Heights neighborhood is fortunate in having much variety, geographic and architectural. The houses run from small to grand, from ugly to handsome. The terrain of hilly, circular streets adds personality to the smallest and plainest of domiciles, and determines how one gardens. A resident living on Griffith Park Blvd. for 30 years told me that she bought her lot because of the favorable slope; she knew that her garden would be adequately watered.

Notes From My Journal:
I enjoy seeing the strong sculptural shapes of cacti and succulents—the desert sajuaro, the century plant, the barrel cactus—alongside the lyrical shape of native California bunchgrass. These plants not only utilize the basic semidesert climate of L. A., but also provide a foil for the rounded and scraggy hillsides. The Franklin Heights walk shows these ideas of good terrain management, and also poor management where grass and other nondesert plants are dominant.

■ We begin at the 1926 Shakespeare Bridge on Franklin Ave. between Myra and St. George. The white, lacy, open-arch appearance of the bridge has an anachronistic quality (it is listed as L.A. historic cultural monument No. 126). The Los Feliz School is on the south side of the bridge; the ABC

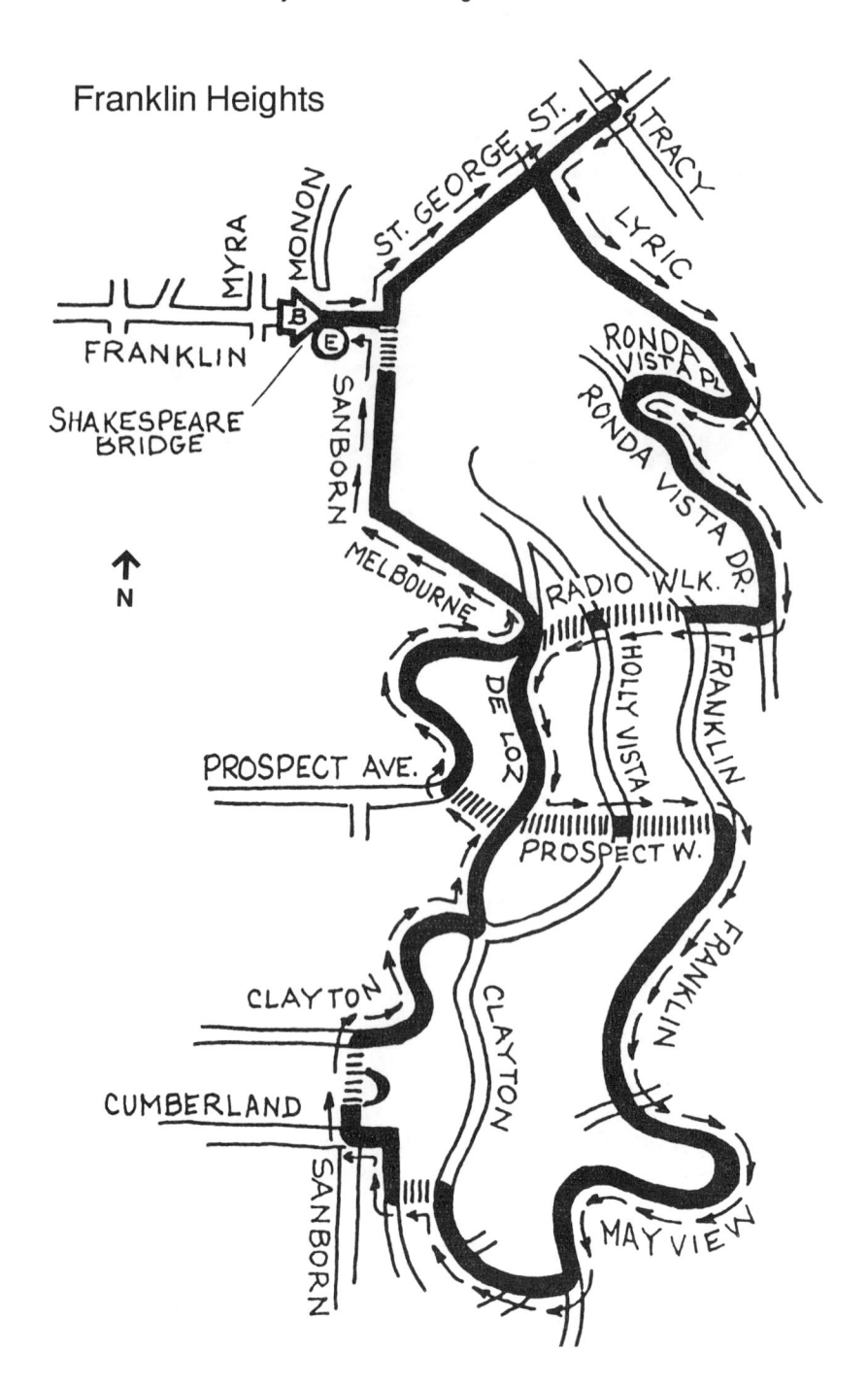

Franklin Heights

Studios are to our right and a hillside of palm trees and houses is below us.

■ Turn left on St. George. John Marshall High School, a brick, half-Gothic structure, is on the northeast corner of St. George and Tracy. It was due to be closed because it did not meet earthquake code standards, but a feasible alternative was adopted—a new interior plus the old shell which was in good condition. Now we retrace our steps back along St. George St. to Lyric Ave. (2400) and turn left. Across from 2435 is an open area completely covered with ivy.

■ Turn right on Ronda Vista Place, then left on Ronda Vista Dr. Turn right on Radio Walk (2200 N.) Cross Franklin Ave. and descend Radio Walk stairway, a beautiful long shady stairway flanked by oleander, Italian cypress and bottlebrush. Between each two cross streets, the stairway is divided into series of stairs and landings, in a minimalist, rhythmic way. Meanwhile, new vistas continually emerge. Cross Holly Vista Ave. and continue down the stairway to Deloz. Turn left on Deloz Ave. to Prospect Walk stairway. Turn left on Prospect Walk stairway and climb back up to Holly Vista Ave. 1801 Holly Vista is a dark brown house with balconies that are overwhelmingly full of succulents and desert plantings. The accouterments of a true gardener are visible—shelves of redwood pots, clay pots and bedding plants. continue up Prospect Walk stairway to Franklin Ave.

■ Turn right on Franklin Ave. Follow Franklin to Mayview Dr. to see the Griffith Observatory to the northwest. Continue to the intersection of Clayton Ave., where we note the special homes here and an extraordinary view in all directions.

■ Turn right on Clayton and take the stairway next to 3880 down to Cumberland Ave. Turn right on Cumberland and follow it around to Sanborn Ave. Turn right on Sanborn and take the stairway to Clayton Ave. (This is a tricky area to map, with a stairway and a cul-de-sac and a serpentine loop, but fun to walk.) Turn right on Clayton to Deloz Ave. Turn left on Deloz to Prospect Walk stairway, next to 1741, and descend the short section of the stairway to Prospect Ave. As we follow the curve around the bend toward the right (going uphill) to Deloz, a great view of north and west L.A. opens up. A little to the left, north of Radio Walk stairway, is the intersection of Melbourne Ave., which we follow toward the left. Melbourne turns into Sanborn Ave., which we follow to its end. Take the Sanborn stairway to Franklin Ave. to our beginning.

Franklin Bridge

Notes From My Journal:
The Franklin Heights Walk was an exciting one to explore because we found so many equivocal sections—we could go this way or that—and we found sections of special interest that would not blend into a coherent walk. What to do—design three walks, two walks, or three in one? While Gene Smith was mapping a three in one, we discovered the Pegasus shape to the walk! It is an intriguing form. We always look for a shoe or a boot shape to our walks; they portend very good walks. Pegasus adds another dimension—possibly a flying, leaping walk.

Franklin Addendum Walk

Rating: $1/2$ Orange

■ The reason for the walk addendum here is our discovery of a superb structure, Villa Giuseppi, at 3431 Waverly Drive. It was designed in 1927 by my favorite California architect, Bernard Maybeck (1862-1957), for Earl C. Anthony, then owner of the Packard agency and radio stations KHJ and KECA. In 1950 Anthony sold the estate to Daniel and Bernadine Murphy Donahue, who gave the 9-acre estate to the Sisters of the Immaculate Heart of Mary in 1970. It is now used as a novitiate and motherhouse and retreat house.

■ My first impression of the Anthony villa was disbelief—all this room for two adults and a child? My second impression was, How fanciful and romantic. Maybeck utilized motifs of Renaissance architecture such as carved designs on doors and downspouts, turrets, and unexpected nooks for solitude. Day retreats are available and tours are given from time to time. Telephone The Immaculate Heart of Mary for information. (213) 664-1126.

■ The original gardens at the villa were designed by Mark Daniels, a gifted landscape architect who planned the total layout—home sites, stairways, gardens and curving streets with ornamental urns—of the beautiful Forest Hills neighborhood in San Francisco (1912) that I love to explore.

■ Walk south on Griffith Park Blvd. from the intersection of Los Feliz Blvd. Turn left on Rowena and turn left again on Waverly Dr. Across from 3412 is the 9 acre plot of Villa Giuseppi. It is best to call ahead for permission to walk through the grounds.

■ Continue on Waverly, then make a right turn on Maxwell St., which becomes St. George St.,and walk to Griffith Park Blvd. Detour left to 2906-2912 to see a most charming bungalow court built in 1925. Reminiscent of Norman cottages, the units have pitched shake roofs and stucco-and-wood construction. A brick walkway pulls one onward toward a planted area in the center and to the rear bungalow, which has a white stucco tower topped with an ingratiating dunce cap roof and weather vanes. Architecturally, this is an oasis. These dwellings are said to have been occupied by Disney artists working in the original Disney studios which were around the corner on Hyperion Ave.

■ Return to the intersection of Griffith Park Blvd. and St. George St. On the southwest corner is the Church of St. Casimir (1951), its doorway, encircled by tiles decorated with religious, historical and nature motifs. St. George on horseback and St. Casimir at a desk with a manuscript are also painted on tile. Casimir (1458-1484) was Prince Of Poland.

■ At this point you can hook into the main Franklin Walk by walking west on St. George to Lyric and turning left. Or if you would rather keep to the addendum outline, walk west on St. George, turn right on Tracy and then right on Ames St. (a delightful area where we see the mailman walking his route wearing headphones). Contractors' sidewalk signatures and dates along the way provide us with an easy index to the development of the area.

■ Continue on Ames to Ben Lomond Pl. and turn right. At Rowena turn right to Griffith Park Blvd. On the corner is a handsome, half-timbered, modified-hip-roof house. The structure behind 3212 Griffith Park is a home masquerading as a fortified castle. A long incline driveway leads to the residence behind the high-angled cement retaining wall with protruding vertical rows of stone. Now continue north on Griffith Park Blvd. to Los Feliz Blvd. to our beginning.

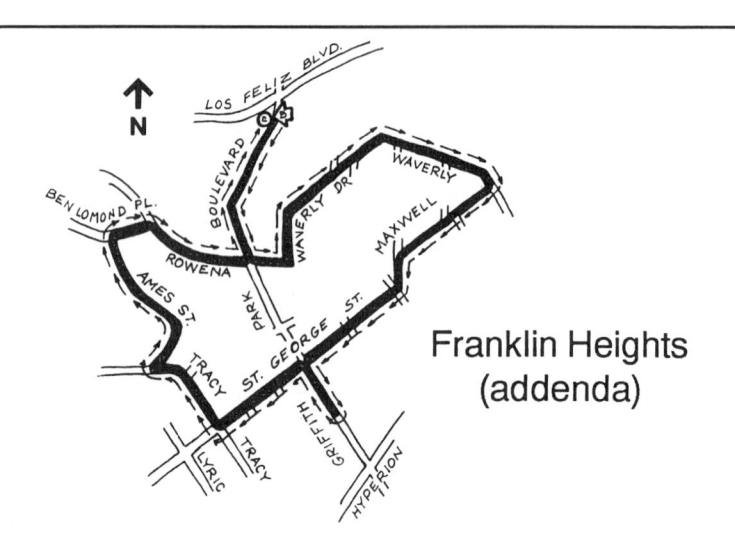

Franklin Heights
(addenda)

Walk 10

LOS FELIZ
Eclecticism Works if All Is in Scale

Boundaries: Los Feliz Blvd., Vermont Ave., Edgemont St.
Rating: 2 Oranges, 2 Figs, 3 Walnuts

■ The Los Feliz neighborhood, high in the hills of northeast L.A. is a choice place to live. It is 15 minutes from downtown L.A. and adjacent to the 4000-acre Griffith Park, the largest municipal park in the United States. Los Feliz was the original Beverly Hills, with stunning views and hillside privacy. Many movie stars resided here in the 1920s and '30s and a few do today. It is also the site of an architectural masterpiece by Frank Lloyd Wright, the Ennis-Brown house, which is on our route.

Notes From My Journal:
The group of 44 settlers from Los Alamos, Sonora arrived in Los Angeles on February 2, 1781, accompanied by Corporal Jose Vicente Feliz and three other military personnel. Their seven-month trip to Upper California was part of a long-range plan for the colonization of this Spanish holding. Governor Neve gave detailed instructions concerning land distribution and design of a town. A formal founding celebration for Nuestra Senora de la Reina de Los Angeles de Porciuncula was held on September 4, 1781. Corporal Feliz, who was a very popular leader, continued to guide the group through the first few years and eventually became owner of Rancho Feliz. Today, Los Feliz Blvd. provides a beautiful entrance to a section of the historic holdings.

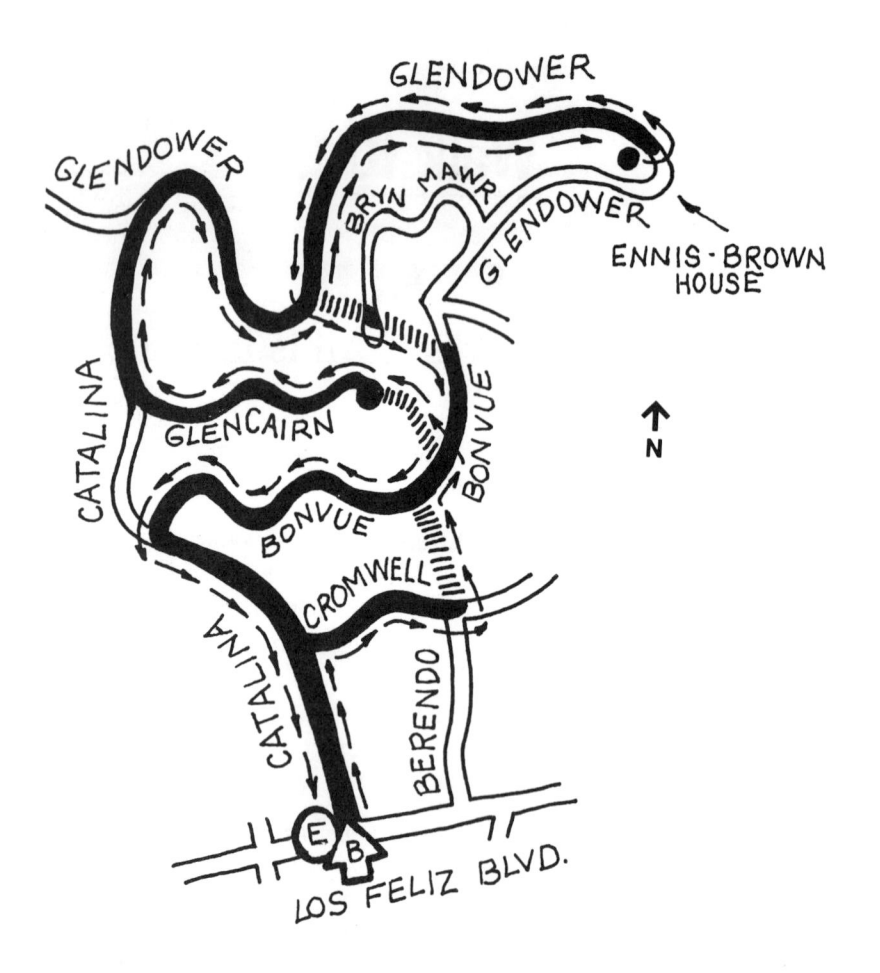

Los Feliz

■ We begin our exploring at Los Feliz Blvd. and Catalina. Walking north on Catalina, we scan an overview: from distant panoramic downtown L.A. to tile-roofed houses on the slopes, to close-ups of ivy and lantana ground cover and an orange tree in the lawn of 230. As we walk we meet the neighbors, eager to share information about their favorite stairways.

■ Turn right on Cromwell to Berendo stairway (next to 4803 Cromwell and across from 2251 Berendo) and ascend. An ornamental concrete lion's head is in the center of the divided stairway. A high wood slat fence is on the left, together with many bamboo trees and ivy—the leaves, three-lobed and layered, make a lovely pattern when back-lit by the sun. Halfway up the stairway is a wide landing with benches and urns, a convenient rest spot with a view. We reach Bonvue across from 4799.

Notes From My Journal:
The Berendo stairway only strengthens my belief that public stairway subscriptions should be used to maintain stairways. The donors would contribute $12 yearly toward maintenance, names and dates would be inscribed on the risers, and the recording of the names would be kept in the city archive office. A subscription would be a great gift for any occasion, and another source of neighborhood and family histories.

■ Turn right on Bonvue past 4791, which has a wall and a view only of the vegetation in the yard. To the right of 4791 is a large multi-angled and balconied three-story pink stucco house. It appears to be on Bonvue, but actually its address is on Glendower. 4781 Glendower (even the number looks like a Bonvue address) is set back on the lot and has a series of patterned cement planters.

■ We cross the street and between 4781 and 4749 Bonvue is a concrete stairway lined with eucalpytus, which we ascend. Here we keep looking back because the views are so grand. At the top, walk through the archway and turn right at the cul-de-sac which is at the end of Glencairn. Walk past 4817 Glencairn, a brick, flat roofed one-level structure surrounded by trees, pyracantha, cactus and jasmine. 4828 has a belvedere allowing a 360-degree view. As we approach 4835 Glencairn, a three-story wood house, we may hear mockingbirds sing among the jacaranda trees. The location of 4840 offers a wide, unobstructed view. Closer at hand stands a Canary Island palm in the backyard of 4885 Glencairn. Follow the curve of Glencairn to Catalina (2500 N.), then turn right.

■ The copper-domed Griffith Park Observatory, built in 1935, is visible from here. It is always a reassuring symbol from whatever neighborhood we see it. Continuing to the fork in the road, we turn right on Glendower past 2829. On our left, adjoining Griffith Park, are sandstone cliffs. Across from 2775 they have been united to prevent slides.

■ We pass by the descending stairway at 2763 Glendower and continue on Glendower in the direction of descending numbers. After we bear right, we reach the Ennis-Brown house, designed by Frank Lloyd Wright in 1924. The wall, ornamented with Mayan designs, begins at 2665 Glendower and continues around the bend. The house, at 2607, is high on a hillside overlooking Olive Hill and the L.A. Basin, and can easily be identified. From the exterior, it is a grandiose Mayan style structure—angular, massive, cinder blocks of grayish color. It has the appearance of a fortress, but from the play of the patterns of the ornamental grillwork gate into the courtyard, we assume that light and reflections from the decorative windows are intrinsic parts of the interior.

■ The house, belonging to the foundation that is overseeing renovation work necessitated by water seepage into the cinder blocks, is on the National Register Of Historic Places, and has been designated as a Cultural Heritage Monument by the L.A. City Council and The Cultural Heritage Board. Public tours are conducted on the second Sunday of January, March, May, July, September and November. Reservations required (213-660-0051).

■ If you want to see an R. M. Schindler home from 1952, walk past the Ennis home to 2567 Glendower. It is stucco, covered with extended roofs. But I find I'm so caught up with the intensity and the drive of the Wright imagination and design that the other homes do not pique my interest.

■ As we turn around and walk back to the left, we do appreciate the scale of the homes built here, which allows room for architectural variety. We continue west along the curve of Glendower until we reach the stairway at 2763. Descend the wide concrete stairway into a cul-de-sac. The stairway has been designed with lovely curves and landings and a nice touch, a lamppost. We hope it's kept in good repair. Continue to the bottom of the stairway where the sign says Bonvue (4700 W.). Turn right on Bonvue, then left on Catalina to Los Feliz, to our beginning.

Notes From My Journal:
Fires in the hills in the dry summer months are normal hazards of view top living. The chaparral—the low-growing shrubs on the rocky hillsides such as mesquite, manzanita, creosote bush and yerba santa—flourish in the aftermath of a fire because of the concentrations of nitrogen and phosphorus in the leaves of the resprouts.

■ **Griffith Park:** North end of Western Ave. north of Los Feliz Blvd. Hours: Daily 5 A.M.-10:30 P.M.

■ **Griffith Observatory and Planetarium:** Hours: Tuesday-Sunday 2-10 P.M.

■ Griffith Park is a wonderful place for an outing—from a simple picnic to a hike of variable length, to a day indoors in the Science Museum or Planetarium. One of my favorite places is the fern grotto, Ferndell, where sycamores and ferns flourish because of a running spring.

Walk 11

LOWER BEACHWOOD
Churches, Temples, Monasteries and Mosques

Boundaries: Gower St., Cahuenga Blvd., Franklin Ave.
Rating: 3 Oranges

■ In the 1920s and 1930s, Hollywood Blvd. was a constant show. Sid Grauman's Chinese Theater, built in 1927, opened with Cecil B. DeMille's *King of Kings*. Grauman's idea of immortalizing the stars in concrete was just right for the high-flinging times. Hollywood Blvd. from Vine to Highland, where young actors awaited their chance, was known as "the street of heartbreaks." The night that prohibition was repealed, December 5, 1933, Hollywood Blvd. was the scene of riotous behavior. Singing and dancing, cavorting and drinking ushered in the new era. The Pig 'n' Whistle restaurant, no longer here, offered its 65-cent blue plate special. Musso and Frank's (still here at 6667 Hollywood Blvd. with its clubhouse seating and warm old-style New York bar atmosphere) offered its varied hot and cold plate specials.

■ A few blocks above Hollywood Blvd., behind today's grungy facades, we come to Beachwood, a stable and tolerant neighborhood where both family and bohemian values are accepted. These values and attitudes are exemplified throughout our walk by the architectural forms and functions of the churches, temples, monasteries and mosques.

■ Begin with a detour (optional) to 1760 Gower St., three blocks east of Vine, between Carlos and La Baig, to see the Hollywood Presbyterian

Church complex which is securely settled into the environment of two-and-one-half city blocks. The Church was formally established in 1903; the first building opened in 1909. School buildings adjoining the church include preschool for ages two and three, a high school, adult classrooms, a family library, a bookstore and a gym. A children's playground and a parking lot complete the complex. Stately pepper trees, hawthorne bushes, Canary Island pines, pittosporum and silk trees are planted in the gardens, irises and azaleas in the courtyard.

Lower Beachwood

■ Our main walk begins at Franklin and Argyle. The walls of the Hollywood Bowl Self Storage Company across the street are vivid with a colorful series of murals relating to Hollywood—portraits and head shots of personalities such as Mickey Mouse, Clark Gable, Elizabeth Taylor and James Dean; in addition, a cityscape with a dollar sign, a crescent moon, and Indian and Egyptian motifs complete the design.

■ Walk east on Franklin St. for one block to Vista del Mar Ave. Turn left on Vista Del Mar for one short and one long block, ascending the beautiful double-arched stairway with the fountain and cactus in the center. In front of us at 6215 Hollymont Dr. a statue of Jesus, an eagle on the landing, Greek figurines and partly broken Corinthian columns provide an incongruous entrance to the Hollymont castle, now used for cultural events. This 31 room abode was once the home of Barbara Stanwyck and husband Frank Fay.

■ Turn left on Hollymont (in front of the Jesus statue) and continue left on Argyle as it goes down the hill. 2041 Argyle is a Spanish style stucco church with an onion top. The building, formerly a Roman Catholic church, is now the home of the Protection of the Holy Virgin Russian Orthodox Church. It was purchased by the congregation, about 200 strong, in 1961. On the Saturday we were there, high-school classes in Russian and religion as well as classes for younger children were in session. Continuing down Argyle, we notice the Hollywood style bungalow-court apartments at 2006, 2014, 2016 and 2027, built around stairways themselves, some fenced for crime protection. On the right at 1953 and 1955 is a charming bungalow court with a terraced stairway, flanked by poplar trees.

■ Toward the bottom of Argyle we turn right on Vine, (technically it is Dix, but the sign says Vine) just above Franklin, and follow it (it now is Vine St.) as it curves up the hill, just next to the freeway. As we climb, we see the Capitol Records building at 1750 Vine St over our left shoulder. Many people think it was designed to look like a pile of phonograph records—but it wasn't.

■ Turn left on Vedanta Terrace and left again on Vedanta Place where the Vedanta Society building is snuggled into a protected area among trees on a small hillock at 1946. The Vedanta Society of Southern California, founded in 1930, offers lectures and classes at no cost, and maintains a temple, a convent and a monastery in Hollywood. The temple, which looks like a small white Taj Mahal, has a lovely room open to the public for meditation. Vedanta teaches that man's true nature is divine, that God exists in everyone, and that the object of our lives is to have this divine nature unfold through much self-effort and self-knowledge. (The contrast between the tranquility and spirituality of the setting and the roar of the freeway next door attests to the complexity of urban living.) The English writer Christopher Isherwood was active in the Hollywood Vedanta Society during the 1940s, and his experiences are the subject of his book *My Guru and His Disciple*.

■ Return to Vedanta Terrace and turn left; then turn right on Ivar Ave., following it as it twists around to Vine St. The barnlike house at 2154 Ivar catches our attention. Turn left on Vine St., then right on Vine Way. At 6282 Vine Way we ascend the stairway. Turn left at the top, on Alcyona.

■ Turn right on Primrose, continuing up the steep street, passing Argyle and bearing right past the intersection of Scenic to Vista Del Mar. Cross the intersection to look at a creche of the Madonna and Child positioned close to 2152 Vista Del Mar. It provides a charming moment on the street among the visible symbols of religious worship from the Far East.

■ Walk over to see the apartment house across the street at 2130 Vista Del Mar, where the Indian guru Krishnamurti lived. Next to it is a secluded and densely foliaged private stairway leading to the Islamic domed house in the back.

■ Now we return to the creche at the intersection, continue north on Vista Del Mar Ave., and then turn right to avoid Vista Del Mar Place. We stop in front of 2244 Vista Del Mar Ave., an English thatch-roofed cottage surrounded by shrubbery and trees, to admire its unity and balance among the other architectural styles. Continue on Vista Del Mar Ave. around the bend to see a series of Islamic houses at 6106, 6107 and 6108. Turn right at Gower, the first intersection. The sign is partly hidden, but be sure to turn there. The Hollywood sign is on our left. We continue down the hill and turn right on Scenic Ave. for a brief detour to see two French-type cottages. At 6111 is a Norman cottage with a small tower attached to the hillside garage. Across the street at 6114 and #6116 is a Hansel-and-Gretel duplex cottage.

■ Return to Gower and walk two blocks down to Carmen Place. Turn right at the Monastery of the Angels and Chapel of Perpetual Adoration.

■ This Dominican cloistered monastery was founded by Mother Mary Gabriel O.P. and four companions in 1924. We were greeted at the door by one of the nuns and learned that baking and selling pumpkin bread is one of their year-round money-raising activities. The recipe was adapted about 30 years ago from the grandmother of one of the nuns. Preparing the dough is physically difficult, and now the monastery has commercial mixers and commercial ovens to accommodate the volume—200 loaves weekly, but during holiday time (Thanksgiving and Christmas) 800 loaves daily. We bought a loaf; it had just the right density and heft which the next morning's eating confirmed. It was a lovely gift to crown a meditative walk, celebrating truth and beauty and the potential of human beings.

■ Turn left on Carmen Ave. and proceed to Franklin Ave. and the start.

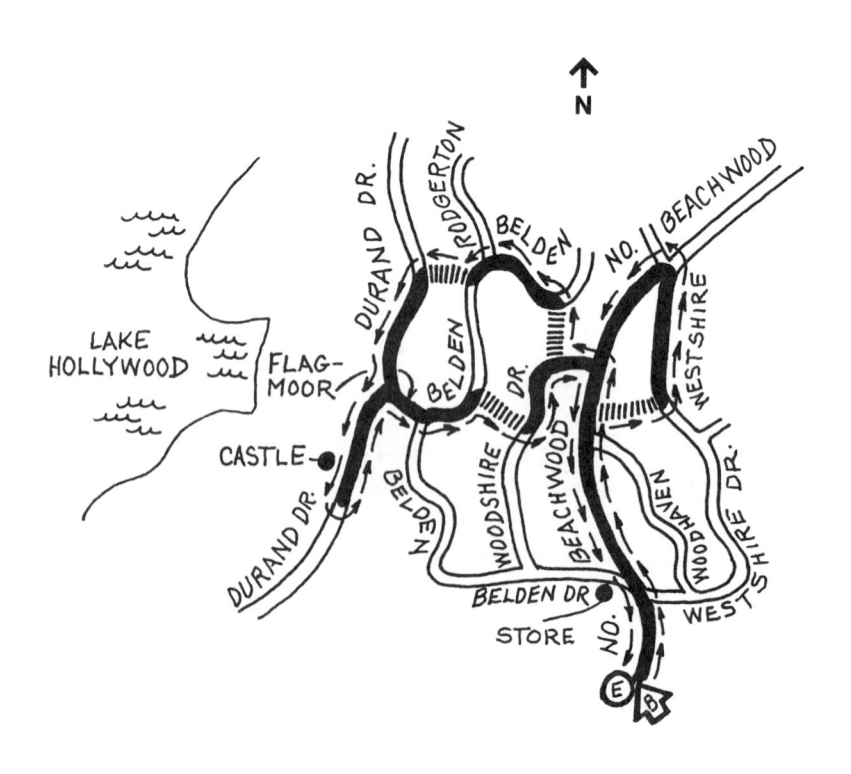

Upper Beachwood

Walk 12

UPPER BEACHWOOD
Castles in the Shadow of the Sign

Boundaries: Beachwood Dr., Belden, Westshire
Rating: 4 Oranges

■ Many people are disappointed to learn that the universal symbol of movie magic—the famous Hollywood sign—had very unglamorous origins. It began in the 1920's as a giant advertisement of what was then a housing subdivision in the Hollywood Hills called Hollywoodland. The project eventually died, the sign eventually fell into disrepair and the last four letters fell down. (Adding to its mystique of gloom, a failed would-be actress hanged herself from the 'H.') Finally, it was adopted by the Hollywood Chamber of Commerce in 1945, minus the last syllable and rebuilt again in 1978. Now its 50 foot high sheetmetal letters are sometimes the scene of collegiate pranks (such as covering up parts of letters to spell a new message) and there are neighborhood fights over proposals to light it at night. However, the sign remains on top of Mount Lee above Beachwood Canyon, dominating the L.A. skyline and symbolizing Hollywood dreams, broken and fulfilled.

■ We head up Beachwood Canyon Drive toward the sign until you reach the two Gothic sandstone gates at Westshire Dr. Those fairy-tale-like towers, now city landmarks, were built in 1923 to be the entrance of Hollywoodland. And, much of what was built behind the gates has a fairy-tale flavor. The six stairways throughout the neighborhood pick up that castle-like theme of granite and black iron. (We will hike four.) The area, furthermore, is dotted with fantasy architecture: Spanish, Moorish, Tudor, French Chateau and, later, spaceship modern. Just inside the gates on our left on the corner of Belden Dr. are a cozy coffee shop/cafe and a grocery store. Inside the store, called the Beachwood Market, are huge blow-up of photos above the freezers on the left. One shows a lovely stairway, with a gurgling fountain in its center. We will be at the real thing in a minute.

■ We stroll back out the store and continue back up Beachwood and take the left turn, which is Woodshire Dr. In about ten feet on our right will be the stairs from the photo. The granite-like facing and black railings are still there, giving it a medieval style, although a visitor wishes it was far better maintained. The fountains were shut off long ago and the little ponds in its center were cemented over, residents explain, because some neighbors complained about the frogs and bugs who took up residence in the water. The ponds now serve as rest-benches, useful because it is a steep climb to the top, where we turn left.

■ We follow what is the upper portion of Belden Dr. around the curve until the first intersection, the one with Rodgerton Dr. Staying to left on Belden, just after the house on the corner and to the right of 2917 Belden is another stairway. This starts out with gentle deep steps and soon turns into another steep stack. However, it is very well cared for by neighbors and has some lovely ivy and wildflowers along side its walls and railings. On top, we pass the classic symbol of hillside Los Angeles life: a private wooden deck with a terrific view of Griffith Park and downtown. Turn left onto what is Durand Dr., walking past homes that are favorite purchases of young screenwriters and directors, past rows of, that incongruous Los Angeles mixture, pines and palm trees.

■ For sightseeing's sake we continue past the sharp turn which is Flagmoor Dr. toward the enormous castle-like wall and gate ahead on the right side of Durand. It is difficult to see from this point, but atop this stern gate is a French-style castle chateau. You might wonder why here? For the answer, continue to follow the castle wall around its base and just to the right of the entrance of 2869 Durand is a surprising and spectacular vista. Below is the sparkling blue waters of Lake Hollywood, the large reservoir built in 1924, and the lush parkland around it. From this spot, paths lead to the concrete bikeway and walkway around the waters edge. You might want to take a detour here for a while but return to this spot by the castle wall and then return toward Flagmoor Dr.

UPPER BEACHWOOD

Woodshire Stairway

■ After retracing our steps for a block, we then walk down Flagmoor until it intersects with Belden, staying to the left on Belden. Three houses after that intersection, just next to 2872 Belden on our right is the top of a charming stairway, lined with iron railings and shaded by thick oleander and hibiscus bushes. We descend, turn left at the bottom and follow what is Woodshire Dr. down to Beachwood again.

■ We cross carefully to the other side of Beachwood at the end of Woodshire Dr. and turn right. The house in front of us, 2810 Beachwood, has the look of an old Spanish Monastery, complete with high walls and second floor verandahs. Just after that house, and before we pass the wooden fence of the next residence, we quickly turn left up another stairway. This one, up to Westshire Dr., has high walls on one side and another castle-like wall at its top.It is cool and shaded but in bad need of repair; so watch your step over some cracks. On top, we stop to look across the canyon and just to the left we can see the French castle which towered above us on Belden. We turn left, walking toward the Hollywood sign, following Westshire Dr. back to Beachwood, where we turn left again and stroll back to the gates of Hollywoodland and perhaps a cool drink at the cafe. (Or, the ambitious hiker might continue north on Beachwood on the tough trails up to the big sign. Beware, however, that the sign is fenced off and police are not kind to trespassers.)

Walk 13

WHITLEY HEIGHTS
Beautiful and Besieged

Boundaries: Highland Ave., Franklin Ave., Hollywood Fwy.
Rating: 0-1 Orange, 2 Plums

■ We park in the lot of the Hollywood Studio Museum at 2100 N. Highland. The structure, originally a barn that Cecil B. DeMille used in the Jesse Lasky Feature Play Company's production of *The Squaw Man*, was moved to its present location at Selma and Vine. Restored by the Hollywood Heritage,Inc. it incorporates DeMille's former office space, including his desk, chair and other accouterments. The barn has been declared California State Landmark 554; and the museum, dedicated to the history of the silent film era in Hollywood, shows silent movies and sells books on film and film posters.

■ The adjoining Whitley Heights neighborhood is a national historic district. Endowed with many pedestrian paths and stairways, it was, during the early days of the film industry the gracious residential area of well-known movie stars, such as Jean Harlow, Gloria Swanson, and Rudolph Valentino. Now it is a besieged area where dogs and 24-hour surveillance signs mark the landscape. The neighborhood is experiencing hostile, threatening and sometimes violent drug-related actions from residents of the floating population of Hollywood Blvd., and in response has installed gates with locks to the stairways.

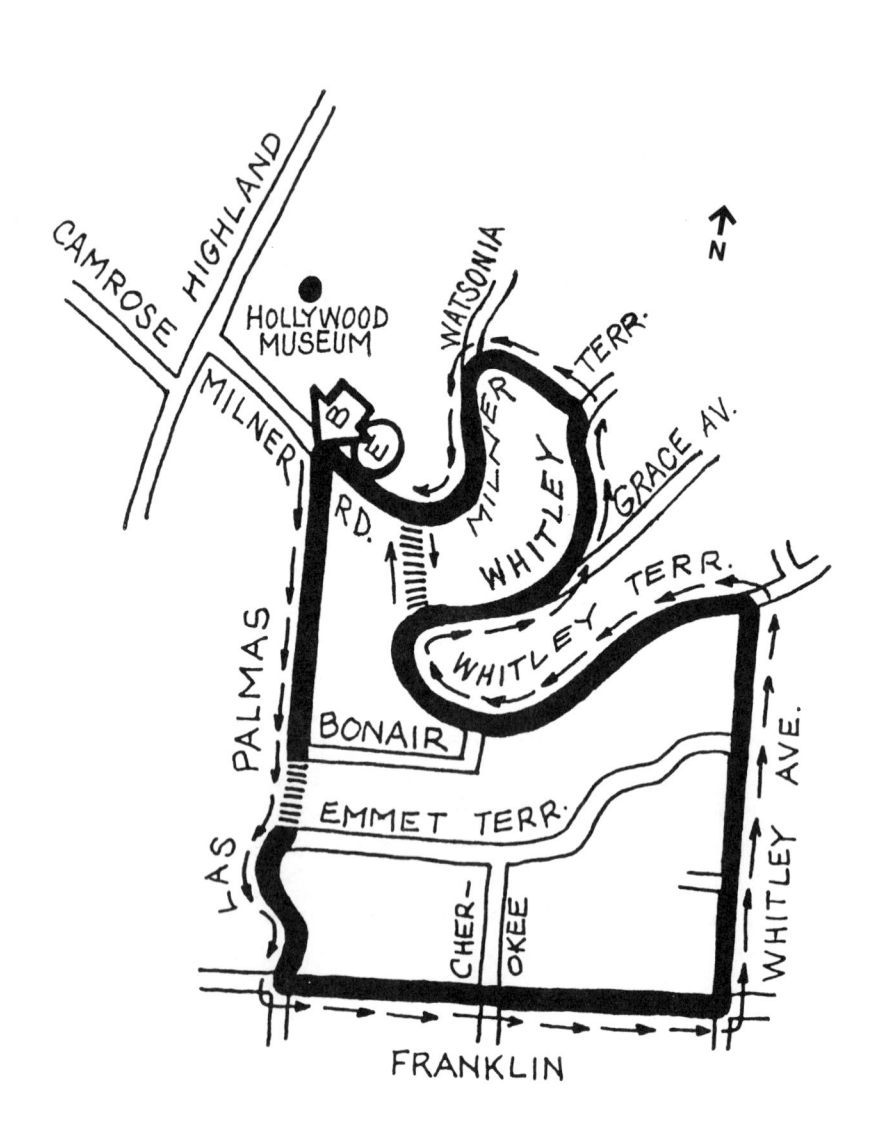

Whitley Heights

■ We begin our walk at Milner and Las Palmas, south of the museum and east of Highland where a whimsical fairy tale house from 1928 is situated on the southwest corner.

■ Go south on Las Palmas. On our left, the multistory houses built on the hillside appear like a Mediterranean village; some have elaborate stairways leading up to them. A bas-relief of a wind-blown woman decorates the entrance of 2006 Las Palmas. Where the street meets Bonair (the sign says 6684 and 6686), we come to the top of a concrete stairway and descend. Continue downhill on Las Palmas past Emmet Terrace (6600 W.) to Franklin. Turn left on Franklin.

■ At 6650 Franklin, near Cherokee St., is the Montecito, an Art Deco apartment tower renovated into senior-citizen housing. Several French-chateau-style apartment buildings from pre-World War II Hollywood are also in this neighborhood.

■ At the next intersection we turn left on Whitley Ave. and then climb up the steep hill. 1929, the Ojai apartments at the corner of Padre Terrace, is another elegant old structure.

■ We turn left on Whitley Terr. and follow as it curves around. Spectacular homes are on our right. 6613 has great Spanish style cathedral windows; 6633 is reminiscent of a Mexican mission; the palazzo across from 6640 has a grand stairway lined with urns. Between 6666 and 6670 Whitley Terr. is the sign for the Whitley Terr. stairway. Its black iron gate is usually unlocked. We descend the zigzag stairway, admiring the old lampposts and peeking into the courtyards and gardens on both sides of the terrace. Ahead of us are fine views of the Hollywood sign and the Santa Monica Mountains.

■ Unfortunately, today the gate at the bottom of the stairway is locked. We can easily hop over the low concrete wall, or we can go back up the stairway and go left at the top gate about 50 feet to where Whitley Terr. splits. Bear left here. The little castle at 6697 has unusual tile murals. Turn left on Milner and walk past Watsonia to our starting point at the parking lot of the museum. Inside, we can visit the exhibits or see a movie.

■ Some architectural structures nearby are worth seeing. The First United Methodist Church at the northwest corner of Highland and Franklin was built in 1929 in an English Gothic style. 1911 N. Highland is a Schindler house built in 1924, and 2000 N. Highland is a lovely garden court apartment house.

Walk 14

HIGH TOWER
Holly, Stars and Visions

Boundaries: Highland Ave., Franklin Ave., Outpost Dr.
Rating: 2 Oranges

■ Harvey Wilcox registered his ranch as "Hollywood" at the survey office in 1887. The name probably came from the proliferation of the California-holly shrub that grew in the hills around the ranch. The climatic conditions that favored this growth were also partly responsible for the gradual emigration of independent film people from the East—semiarid good "shooting" weather year round. In addition the variety of topography and excellent business and real estate opportunities lured these entrepreneurs to Hollywood. (Hollywood was annexed to L.A. in 1910.)
■ Since the early 1900s the name "Hollywood" has been synonymous with the film industry. William Selig built his large studio here in 1909; in 1910 D. W. Griffith brought his Biograph Players from the East; a few years later Thomas Ince, Edwin S. Porter and Cecil B. DeMille arrived. By the 1920s the star system was established, and Hollywood was recognized as the movie producing capital of the world.
■ Exaggeration epitomized the star system. Everything was bigger than life—salaries, houses, parties, and the Hollywood Bowl—one of the largest amphitheaters in the United States, at 2301 N. Highland Ave. Even the history of the Bowl illustrates a cosmic idealism. A group of community-spirited people envisioned the Bowl as the site to present the highest-quality artistic performances to the public. In July 1922, on a

makeshift stage, the Hollywood Bowl opened as the summer home of the Los Angeles Philharmonic. Tickets cost 25 cents.

■ In addition to concerts featuring conductors and musicians like Sir Thomas Beecham, Zubin Mehta, Jascha Heifetz and Joan Sutherland, some once in-a-lifetime performances have been staged at the Bowl. I wish I could have seen *Midsummer's Night's Dream*, directed by Max Reinhardt, and the monumental pageant of 6000 immigrants becoming

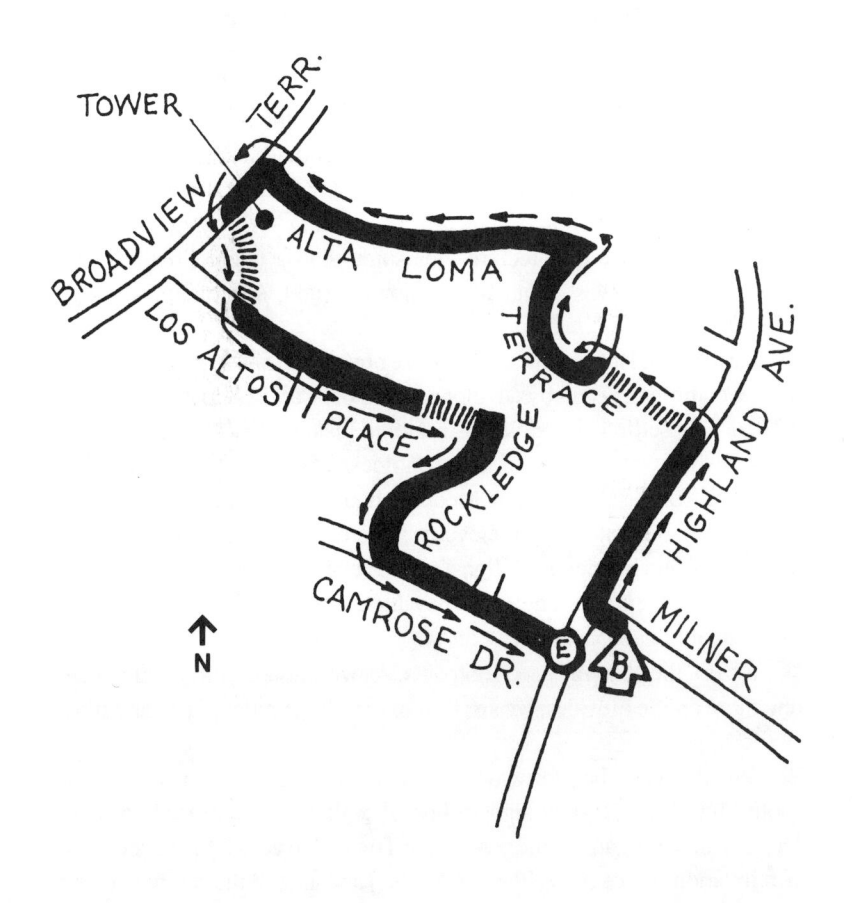

High Tower

U.S. citizens—surely the zenith of publicly shared aspirations for the future. The Theater Arts Alliance has continued to direct the Bowl since its first year. The original impulse of the founders—art for the people—is still pertinent today; the attendance has grown to over 700,000 yearly.

■ We begin our walk at Highland and Milner. Walk north to Alta Loma Terr. the alley way across from the Hollywood Studio Museum and a little north of Camrose Dr. between apartment buildings 2125 and 2139. Turn left into Alta Loma Terr. A stairway is visible with a lovely old wrought-iron lamp at the base. We ascend and find ourselves in a wonderful private world of Spanish-style homes and Japanese gardens. At the top of the stairway, turn right at the walkway intersection. Then, a few houses down facing a fence, turn left. Ahead of us is a long footpath. The setting is so exquisite, with the ice plants, fennel, lantana, aloe, morning glory and pyracantha, that it is difficult to associate it with the deteriorated part of Hollywood and Franklin Blvds. Over our left shoulder are great views of Hollywood's highrises and movie palaces. 6869 and 6881 Alta Loma exemplify Japanese-style architecture. Continuing to Broadview Terr. we see some Moderne architecture plus some that is unclassifiable. 2200 Broadview Terr. was designed by Lloyd Wright, son of Frank Lloyd Wright.

■ Turn left on Broadview Terr. We are now in the highly romantic High Tower community built by developer-architect Carl Kay in the 1920s and 1930s. This setting is popular with movie makers and actors, both as a place to live and a place to shoot movies. Directly in front of us, in delightful contrast to the sleek Moderne houses is High Tower (1920), a rectangular Bolognese-style elevator structure that overlooks the City. The 30 resident members of High Tower Elevator Association pay for the Tower's maintenance, and only they have keys to the elevator, which takes them to garages below.

■ We use the stairways and footpaths. As we wander a bit, looking here and there on the hillsides, we see bird of paradise, spider plants and lilies of the Nile.

■ We descend the stairway that passes next to the Tower and its footbridge. Turn left at the sign for Los Altos Place and walk to Hightower Drive, where we can see the base of the Tower. Go across the street to the continuation of Los Altos Place (6800 W.) and ascend the stairway to the street called Rockledge Road (2100 N.) Among the Spanish-style homes is a peach-colored castle at 2144, perched on the north side. Follow

High Tower

Rockledge as it snakes its way in an **S** pattern down to Camrose Dr. Turn left and walk back out to Highland to our beginning.

■ If you want to see the Hollywood Bowl, turn left on Highland to Hollywood Bowl Rd. The Hollywood Bowl Museum, which is on the grounds, should be visited first. Opened in 1984, it is a delightful place with its priceless memorabilia and archives of the Bowl.

Walk 15

UCLA
Treeing Around the Campus

Boundaries: Sepulveda Blvd., Wilshire Blvd., Beverly Glen Blvd, Sunset Blvd., Gayley Ave.
Rating: 2 Oranges

■ It is sometimes possible to park on Hilgard near Strathmore Ave. where we begin the walk. If not, continue south on Hilgard for a few yards to the Westholm entrance to a parking lot. At the information booth, we are given a token in exchange for $4, which allows us to park all day. Park in parking structure 2, which is closest to the beginning of our walk.

■ Edward A. Dickson and Dr. Ernest Carroll Moore, fervent supporters of a southern campus in the University of California system, were bitterly opposed by President Wheeler of UC Berkeley, the Board of Regents and members of the legislature. In 1900 the odds were great that UCLA would be only an imaginary campus. By 1929, after years of prodigious efforts to overcome vested interests, Dickson and Moore had established and built the Westwood campus of UCLA, the last transformation of L.A. Normal School, founded in 1881.

■ A vibrant institution with excellent academic reputation, UCLA has, more or less, 35,000 students, 3000 faculty, 1800 teaching and research assistants, and 17,000 nonacademic personnel. It is a gem in the UC system, and one of the most pleasant domains in the Westwood village neighborhood where it accounts for almost everybody who looks college age in the block-long lines at the movie houses; and in the overflow of

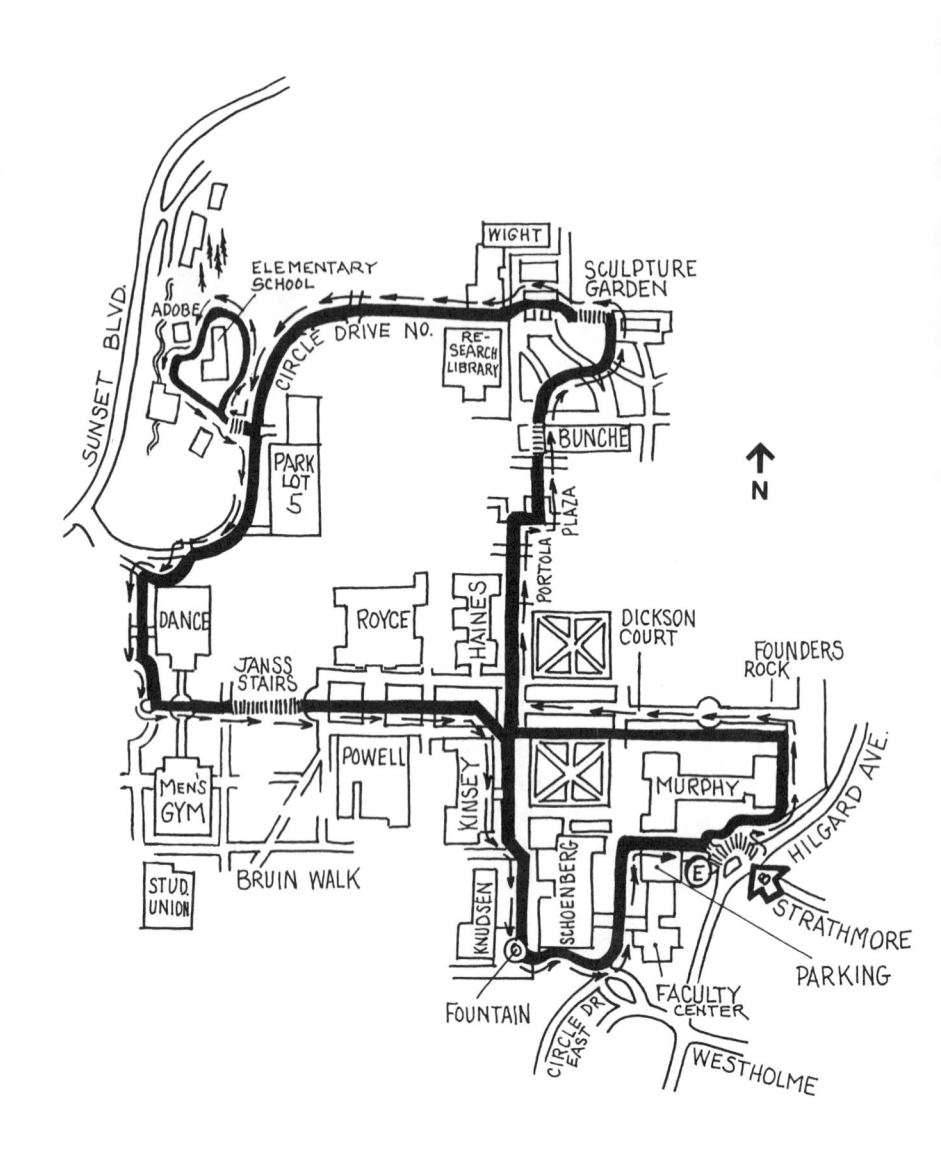

UCLA

diners at the restaurants. In the midst of this enormously energetic atmosphere, we can still take a quiet walk via stairways through some of the school's 411 acres. Tree specimens from around the world are an important feature of the campus, complementing the architecture and the grand layout of the spaces.

■ On our walk we learn the names of people who are important links to the early history of the campus—Dickson, Moore, Janss, Royce and Murphy. We think about their contributions as we begin our exploring at the intersection and major bus stop of Strathmore and Hilgard Ave. (on the east side of the campus.) Walk up the stairway into the campus, and make an immediate right turn into Murphy parking lot. Continue toward the right. We walk on the macadam until we come to the sidewalk on the left side. Continue on the sidewalk to see Founder's Rock; walk north to approach and touch.

Notes From My Journal:
In 1923, Edward Dickson, co-founder of UCLA and one of my favorite L.A. historic characters, and Irwin Muma looked out over the rancho of John Wolfskill, stood on what is now Founder's Rock, and said, "this is it" (or words to that effect). They visualized a great university campus in the center of the area, and a beautiful college town surrounding it. The new UCLA campus was formally dedicated on what is now Dickson Court on October 25, 1926.

■ Turn left on Dickson Court and walk on the right-hand sidewalk. Photogenic Moreton fig trees line the court. Continue west toward the flag pole in front of Haines Hall, one of the original four buildings on the UCLA campus. Walk north on Portola Plaza. Pass Campbell Hall on the left, and continue on the brick walkway that leads to the stairway of Bunche Hall. Dr. Ralph Bunche was one of two Nobel Laureates from UCLA. He was a Summa Cum Laude graduate, 1927, a football star, and later our ambassador to the United Nations.

■ We ascend the stairway and walk through the courtyard to the Murphy sculpture garden. Stopping at the top of the stairway we relish the beauty of the intriguing Hong Kong Orchid trees planted on either side, a prelude to the visual enticement of the garden. Ahead of us, and in the center of the courtyard, is Jacques Lipchitz' powerful and evocative "Song Of Vowels," the first acquisition for the Garden. (Norton Simon contributed toward the purchase, and many of the other pieces came from the collection of David Bright, a Beverly Hills industrialist.) We see on the left "Standing Woman" by Gaston Lachaise. (Marsden Hartley was right when he described her as "goddess of fecundity—entire universe in the form of a woman.") Peter Voulkos' "Gallne Rock" is just ahead and to the left.

■ Make a sharp right turn at the end of the footbridge and follow the path to the left toward the front of the reflecting pool. Coral trees have been planted in the Square. Looking up, I am charmed and bewitched by the two bronze columns about 6 feet high of bas-relief dancing figures. On the top of each column is a delicate nude female dancer, balancing one foot on the cone and holding onto the other foot. These two fine pieces were sculpted by Robert Graham. A bold water sculpture by George Tsutakawa resides in the rectangular pool.

■ Walk up the stairway to the left. A Henry Moore piece is the compelling presence in the coral- tree- lined promenade in front of Macgowan Hall. Walk left to the Wight Art Gallery (if you can go in, do so; their exhibits are small in scale, but choice.) Pass "Torso" by Maillol on the left. Continue west on the path between the gallery and the research library, down to Circle Drive N. The Ralph Cornell Grove, honoring the original landscape architect and designer of the UCLA campus is on the right, on the grounds of the chancellor's house. After the intersection, walk on the right hand sidewalk of Circle Drive N. to the stairway opposite parking lot 5.

■ Descend to the Corinne A. Seeds University Elementary School grounds. What a lovely wooded area! It is a totally different environment from the stately buildings and predictable albeit beautiful walkways of the "upstairs" campus. The indoors and outdoors are a continuum—collages, drawings and clay figures on the walls of the porticos and classrooms, picnic tables and benches, play equipment, trees and water. They all convey the implicit message of Stone Canyon oasis—enjoyment of learning.

■ The school, in existence since 1882, is an internationally renowned experimental research school for the Graduate School of Education. It is now being threatened with the loss of its location (UCLA wants to build a Graduate School of Management on the wooded 9 acres) and its independence. Parent groups are opposing this plan.

■ Turn right on the path to the Peter Mueller Redwood Forest, named for the gardener who tended the plantings for 37 years. Turn left at the west end of the school building on the left of the grove. Turn left again past a small adobe structure on the right side of the school patio. Turn left in back of the adobe along the path that follows the creek through the

Janss Stairway

redwoods and ferns, and continue on the path to the wooden bridge. The school is built above the creek, which does not allow us an exit, so return to the stairway opposite parking lot 5 by walking through the passageway between the library and the kindergarten and ascend it.

■ Turn right and continue walking past the new Bower Museum until you come to the end of the dance building. Turn left on the sidewalk between the dance building and the men's gym. This leads us to the Janss stairway.

Notes From My Journal:
The Janss brothers, Dr. Edwin and Harold, through the Westwood Investment Corporation, developed the Westwood area between Wilshire Blvd. and UCLA. It was annexed to L.A. in 1926. Both men believed in the idea of a southern campus, and in 1924 they bought the land on which UCLA stands from the Arthur Letts estate. Through a generous gift of tax credits, they donated it to UCLA. One of their additional gifts of $50,000 paid for the campus gate at Westwood and LeConte Avenues, and the 18-foot-long red-brick Janss stairway leading from Royce Hall to the men's and women's gymnasiums. The stairway has traditionally been the locale for campus rallies, including the historic ones for Adlai Stevenson and Martin Luther King. The top of the Janss stairway is a lovely place to view a sunset.

■ Then up, up, up the stairway through the quadrangle of the original buildings of UCLA—Royce, Powell, Haines and Kinsey, to the Flagpole, the geographic center of the campus (the Moreton bay fig tree is just right of it).

Notes From My Journal:
Standing at the Flagpole, I imagine myself in the 1850s. From the arroyo between what is now the Flagpole and Murphy Hall, lined with beautiful live oaks and sycamores, I see jackrabbits and black-tailed deer in the distance, frolicking in the meadows.

■ Turn right on Portola Plaza and walk past Knudsen Hall. A sound, alternately soothing and tumultuous as from a flowing mountain stream, comes from the Inverted Fountain a few yards away, designed by Jere Hazlett in 1973. The inversion adds mystery to the sound. That, and the freedom to sit and allow the water to run over my hands and feet, makes this one of my favorite stops on the campus. From the fountain, follow the path due east down a few stairs. Turn left on Circle Drive E. On the right pass the faculty center and a parking lot. At the first intersection turn right on the sidewalk to the stairway we originally walked up, and descend to the bus stop.

Notes From My Journal:
I wish the UCLA Bookstore would sell campus pop-ups to induce the reverie that connects past to present. From walking on land that was valued at 35 cents an acre when Don Alanis raised cattle and horses in the 1820s to walking on the same land valued today at $750,000 an acre calls for screeching mental accommodation.

People Behind the Name Behind the Building

■ Royce Hall, designed by David Allison (1928-29) and modelled on the Basilica of San Ambroglio in Milan is probably the most easily recognized building on the UCLA campus. Josiah Royce was the first Professor of Philosophy at UCLA.

■ Powell Hall, the undergraduate library, was named for Lawrence Clark Powell, retired chief librarian and founder of the School of Librarianship, a noted bookman and bibliographer. The building, designed by architect George W. Kelham(1928), has an octagonal tower, and a doorway modeled after the Cathedral of Verona. The dome resembles the dome of St. Pepolcro in Bologna. Inside the dome is, I think, a most imaginative salutation to the history of reading—the marks of 40 great printers.

■ Moore Hall of Education, south of Powell Hall, was named for the co-founder and first president of UCLA, and former president of L.A. State Normal School. *Kigela pinnata*, the odd looking sausage tree, related to the trumpet vine, reposes in the lawn. Its leaves are a brownish maroon color due to the paucity of bats to pollinate the tree. The walkway has nice detail of stone squares patterned in arcs.

■ Dickson Art Center is named for the co-founder of UCLA. He received his B.A. at Berkeley, then went to Japan to teach while working on his M.A. thesis. Through the carelessness of dock-workers, his trunk with all his notes sank in Yokohama harbor. He returned to the states, took a newspaper job, and became editor of the *L.A. Express* at the age of 38. Gradually, through step-by-step involvement in community affairs, including appointment as a UC Regent, he was able to garner community and state support for UCLA. (I value the amendment he wrote to the California State Constitution in 1910-1911 giving women the right to vote.)

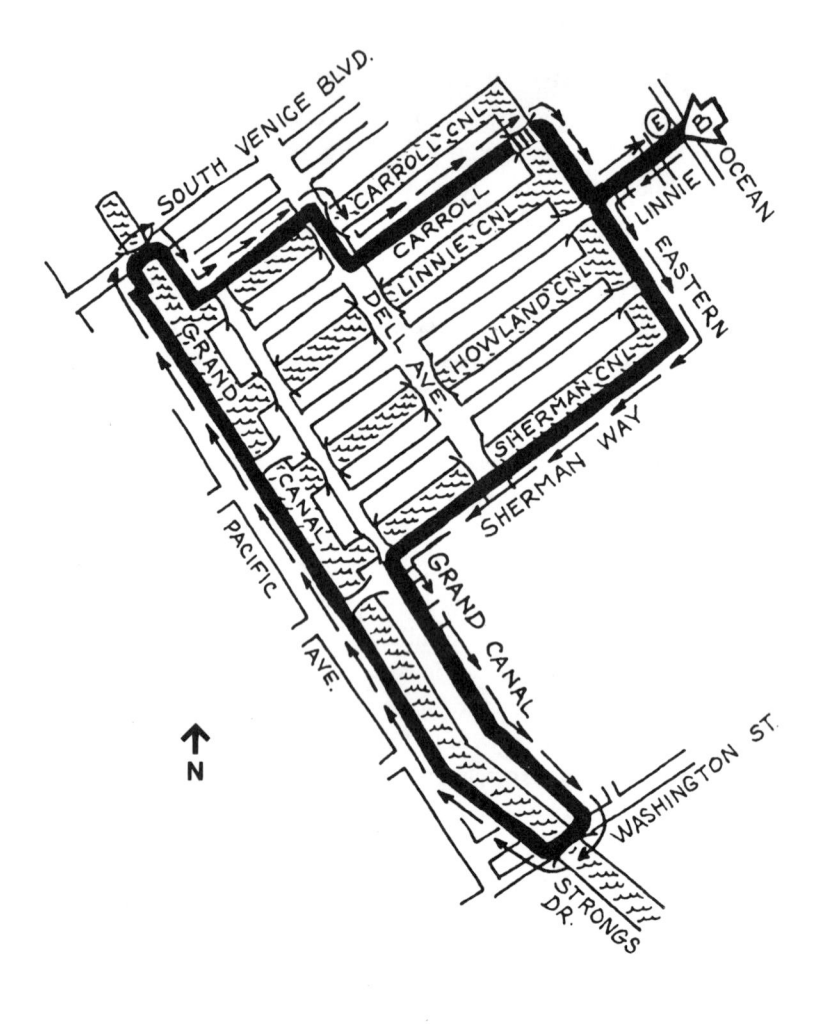

Venice

Walk 16

VENICE
Divertissement—Beware the Mallard Doo

Boundaries: Washington St., Pacific Ave., Venice Blvd, Ocean Ave.
Rating: 1 Orange, 3 Pineapple Guavas

■ Venice—Italy or California. A.D. 400 or A.D. 1904. The only connections between them are the name and the dream of Abbot Kinney, who studiously built canals and gondolas and equivalent architecture in his New World Venice. Now the canals are almost dried up; the gondolas are gone, and architectural eclecticism startles the pedestrian.

■ There is no mistake: this is Venice, California, probably the most interesting and complex beach town along the southern California coast. Some of its history and flavor has been preserved for us in the film *Number Our Days* (1977) by Barbara Myerhoff, a wonderfully warm anthropological study of the lives of elderly Jews whose days revolve around the politics and activities of the Israel Levin Senior Adult Center.

■ Our stairway walk will circumnavigate the old canal area and the bridge walkways. The atmosphere around the canal area is in one sense makeshift, easy- going, casual—mallards have their rights. I approve.

■ The famous Venice amusement park has been demolished, but some remnants of the past can be seen at Ocean and Windward—the original arched buildings now housing stores and restaurants, and the Venice theater, which many people want to restore. Today, vendors sell their wares from open stalls at Ocean Front Walk, and people cavort on roller skates in the cemented area.

■ We begin at Linnie Ave. and Ocean Ave. Small cottages line both sides of the half-block walk to the beginning of the bridge, where we turn left on the footpath of Eastern Canal. We watch our step because the path is uneven and jagged. The water in the canal is stagnant, but the coots and the mallards are swimming about comfortably, and are present in cocktail-party numbers.

■ Pass Howland Bridge, a footbridge with half-inch slats for steps, just for pedestrians. The canals give the area a playful feeling; they are a *divertissment*. They are also landmarks, listed on the National Register of Historic Places. On the other side of the water is a huge stand of pampas grass, a botanical pest that crowds out native plants.

■ Continuing our walk along the outline of the canal system, we turn right on Sherman Canal. Here we don't have to imagine honking mallards in front yards and mallard doo all over the walkways; it is the prevailing condition. At Dell Ave. we note a miscellany of objects: a blue tile roof, windmills, boats, fake flamingos, a stone bench and hanging on the side of a house, Dutch shoes. Broken sidewalks are also part of the landscape.

■ Venice is in the early stages of large-scale renovation of the waterways. The sign nearby says, "Venice Canal rehabilitation armoflex pilot test plot." The purpose of the experiment is to determine how feasible the armoflex material is as a plant container for growing and preserving food for the small fish.

■ Farther along, the area looks less cluttered. Windows are decorated with plants, and an unexpected gazebo stands nearby. Continue on Sherman Canal past Dell Ave. At the end of Sherman Way, turn left to walk on the east side of Grand Canal to Washington. Houses are in good condition in this section. Turn right on Washington to Strongs Drive, where you can stop for a lunch break at one of the neighborhood restaurants. Then return to walk northwest on Strongs Dr. on the left bank (west side) of the Grand Canal.

■ Along the way, we see charming vignettes that predispose us to an easygoing state of mind—a highly active gull-landing field, close to a solitary boat resting under a mock orange tree, not far from a blooming hawthorne tree and a Chinese magnolia, near congregations of male and female mallards looking like plants in a still life. Meanwhile, watch out for the —.

Notes From My Journal:
Pig Turd Alley is a street in Amador City, California.

■ Today, the air resounds with much house repair activity. The series of cottages on the even numbered side have small lawns, and the balconies are in the style of early California architecture. Continue on the west bank of Grand Canal (2604), passing the 27th Ave. bridge, a wooden stairway bridge, and Sherman Way. We keep to the outline of the canal system. There are four branches off the Grand Canal: Carroll, Linnie, Howland and Sherman. A footbridge just north of Howland extends from the east bank to the west bank.

■ Walking beside the waterway we sight, across the canal, a night heron standing in the top of a large flame tree, and in the canal the reflections of a blue-bottomed white rowboat with red stripes painted down the sides. Clumps of pickleweed and houses designed with porthole windows which extend the sea-going atmosphere, are on our route as we pass Linnie Canal.

■ Arriving at S. Venice Blvd. we walk up the stairway to the bridge. The sign at the top of the stairway "you have entered a water bird sanctuary," reminds us of the delicate balance here between the silted canals on one side and the endangered least tern and salt marsh skipper butterfly on the other. (In the latest plan, the canals will be preserved as wetlands, and additional vegetation like pickleweed and salt grass will be planted.) Turn right to the stairs and walk on the wooden sidewalk. Then descend to the east side of the canal and walk south. Turn left and walk on the north side of Carroll Canal, where you'll find heavenly bamboo, hibiscus and magenta ice plant. Someone planted asparagus fern along the canal as well as geraniums, thus providing a nice contrast to the brick walkway,

■ Turn right on Dell Ave. and cross the concrete auto bridge to the south side of the canal and turn left. On the northeast corner of Dell and Carroll is a timber-and-stucco French-style cottage with a tower, an undulating shingle roof and stained-glass windows. Near 425 Carroll is a castor bean plant and aloe. There are many large homes here and some new, attractive homes of various styles, including Moderne. Palm trees line the way.

■ Continue east on the right side of Carroll to Eastern Canal (which parallels Grand Canal). Turn right on Eastern Canal. Walk over the footbridge to the east side of the canal. North of Linnie stands a beautifully maintained, large, light-yellow wooden house with porches. Across from it is another large home with a gabled dormer window, a wrap-around

Carroll Canal

porch and a fenced-in dock which is used as an enlarged play area over the canal for the children. Nearby is a day care center. Turn left on Linnie to complete the outline of the canal system.

■ There are going to be many changes in the physical appearance of Venice. A consensus is finally being reached among the various groups (the California Coastal Commission, environmental groups, and boat owners) on how best to renovate Venice's canals in a sound ecological way, and yet accommodate special interests.

Notes From My Journal:
Abbot Kinney's first development was Ocean Park; Venice was next. In 1921 he planted eucalyptus along Rustic Canyon to find out which species would survive the coastal climate.

■ Addendum: the Los Angeles City Council has approved the proposal to reline 3 $1/2$ miles of canals with concrete blocks, which will promote the growth of native vegetation and at the same time permit the necessary tidal cleansing. The California Coastal Commission has authority to make the final decision on the efficacy of the "demonstration project."

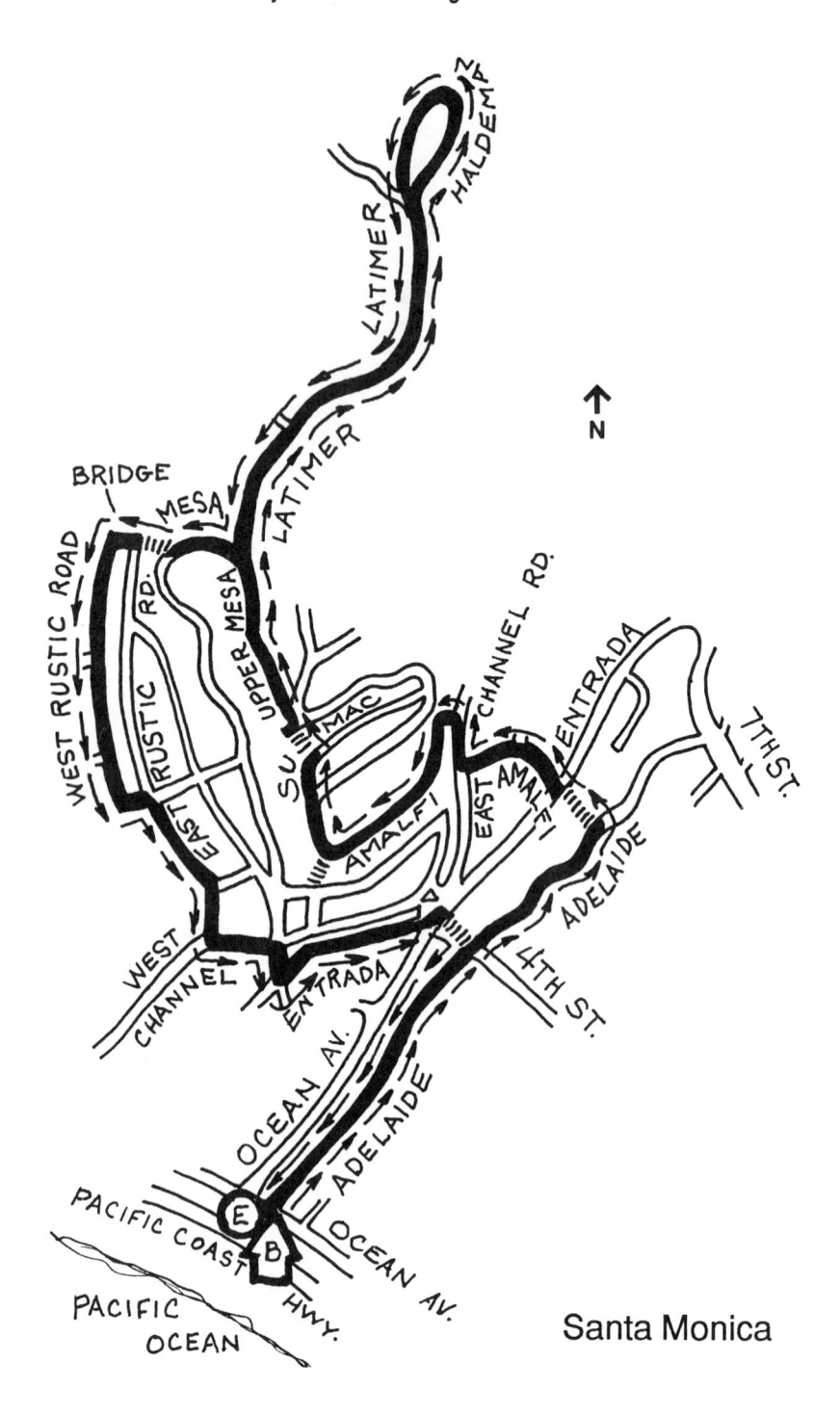

Santa Monica

Walk 17

SANTA MONICA
Sea Breezes and Clear Air, but Watch For Street Angles

Boundaries: Pico Blvd., Sunset Blvd., Chatauqua Blvd., Pacific Coast Hwy.
Rating: 2 Oranges, 3 Pistachio Nuts

■ The name "Los Angeles" can evoke a simple Pavlovian response—images of freeways and automobiles. But L.A. is complex. It includes the Santa Monica Mountains National Recreation Area which is visited by 27 million people annually and consists of 55 miles of seashore and mountain weaving around the city and encompassing a range of ecosystems. We will explore two lovely neighborhoods near the national recreation area, Rustic Canyon and the cliff side section of Santa Monica. These areas have a special atmosphere of relaxation, of people taking time to walk and to look.

■ The city of Santa Monica was founded in 1875, and from its early days to the present it has been a desirable place to live. It had a busy harbor (now superseded by San Pedro), and potential residents arrived via steamer from San Francisco eager to participate in land sales. In 1887, the Arcadia Hotel, one of the most elegant on the Coast, opened for business on Ocean Ave. between Colorado and Pico. People came to enjoy the sea breeze, the clear air and the beautiful beach. The red interurban electric trolleys provided more impetus for growth during the early 1900s (the commute time from downtown L.A. was 30 minutes).

■ Today, Santa Monica, sometimes called the "Peoples' Republic of Santa Monica," is a political town with strict rent controls. It also places a high priority on public landscaping. Palisades Park is an inviting and popular place to sit and enjoy the views and the flowers.

■ We begin our walk at Ocean Avenue (100) and Adelaide Dr. (100), at the corner where the penthouse at 101 Ocean overlooks the water.

■ Turn right on Adelaide. Silhouettes of the sugar-gum eucalyptus and the Torrey pine enhance a breathtaking view of Santa Monica Canyon on our left. February is a most propitious month for the senses. Everything is in bloom, or almost in bloom. Date palms are bursting, the hawthorne hedges are pink, wild radish and fennel are growing along the sides of the road. Across the canyon are two large patches of magenta ice plant and bouganvillea.

■ We might see a practice mountain rescue performed by the fire department across the street from 406 Adelaide. A dummy is pulled up from the canyon on a stretcher, slowly and carefully, while a video camera records the efforts for playback and critique at the firehouse.

■ The homes on Adelaide are custom built, mostly amalgams of different traditional styles, among them California ranch, modified pueblo, and Arizona desert. They are made from a variety of materials, including brick, wood and plaster, and they occupy spacious lots. They are attractive and eye-catching by virtue of their mass and their well designed landscaping. Walk down the wooden stairway across from 526, where a lemonade sumac is growing.

Notes From My Journal:
At 7th St. and Adelaide, where 7th dips into the canyon, Ysidro Reyes built the first adobe house in Santa Monica, in 1839. It was destroyed in 1906.

■ Along the sides of the stairway, in addition to the king palm in which two mockingbirds are singing, beavertail cactus, sorrel, hawthorne, mock orange, sage, rosemary and acacia are interspersed, converting the space to a wildlife sanctuary which is overgrown and taken for granted. There is a middle landing, so we can stop and appraise the views and look at the ridge separating Santa Monica Canyon from Rustic Canyon. We continue down the stairway section. On the next landing we talk with some other walkers coming up the stairway. The final group of wooden stairs takes us to Entrada Drive (400 N.).

■ We cross Entrada, walk to Amalfi Drive (100) and turn left. On the left side, in the center of the playground at Canyon School, are two standing walls with murals of a house and trees. Turn right on East Channel Road (400 N.) (The canal has a runoff of water from the hills). Now turn left on Amalfi Dr. Looking across the canyon from 237 Amalfi, we see the Fourth St. stairway, which we will be walking on later. Between 271 and 275 Amalfi Dr. is a walkway and stairs down to Sage Lane (mental note to explore another time).

■ We continue on Amalfi Dr. into Sumac Lane (300 N.) and ascend the stairway next to 323 Sumac. It has a concrete and iron railing, and a series of stairs and landings. It has a beautiful profile among the vegetation, and the lighting gives it a chiarioscuro mysterious quality.

■ At the top turn left on Upper Mesa Road (400 N.) and walk downhill. Then turn right into Latimer Road (500 N.)—and remember to watch for street angles. We are now in Rustic Canyon, still part of L.A. A few yards beyond the intersection of Hilltree Rd. (4600 W.) on the left side of the street near the recreation center is a plaque. It commemorates the establishment in 1887, of the first experimental forestry station testing exotic trees for planting in California. Various sport activities for children are in progress at the center, as well as painting and ceramic classes for adults. The outdoor picnic area is pleasant, and we can sit and watch the children.

■ As we leave the patio of the recreation center we bear right on Haldeman. (Sometimes the wooden sign is down.) Originally, Rustic Canyon was a private club. Now the streets are owned by the member-homeowners, and they assess themselves for maintenance of the roads, the signs, and the berms to slow down traffic. There are no sidewalks or curbs. One of the first houses in Rustic Canyon at the corner (2 Latimer) was owned by Johnny Weissmuller, and later by Lee Marvin. Many of the early residents were in the entertainment industry; now most are in the professions.

■ Continue on Haldeman—that is, if you are walking on the right-hand side. Here is the story: the numbers on the right side are two-digit, and the post-office address is Haldeman; the numbers on the left side are one-digit, and the post-office address is Latimer! and we're still in L.A. The log cabin residences at 36 and 37 Haldeman are purported to come from a movie set. At 8 Latimer we turn left to loop around, walking downhill and passing Rustic Canyon cooperative nursery school and the fronts of the houses we've been seeing from the back. We especially enjoy 7, an English style with a shake roof and a chimney built of river stones. Continue on Latimer back to Mesa Rd. Turn right on Mesa. (500 N.) At the side of 491, descend the stairway that takes us across the bridge to

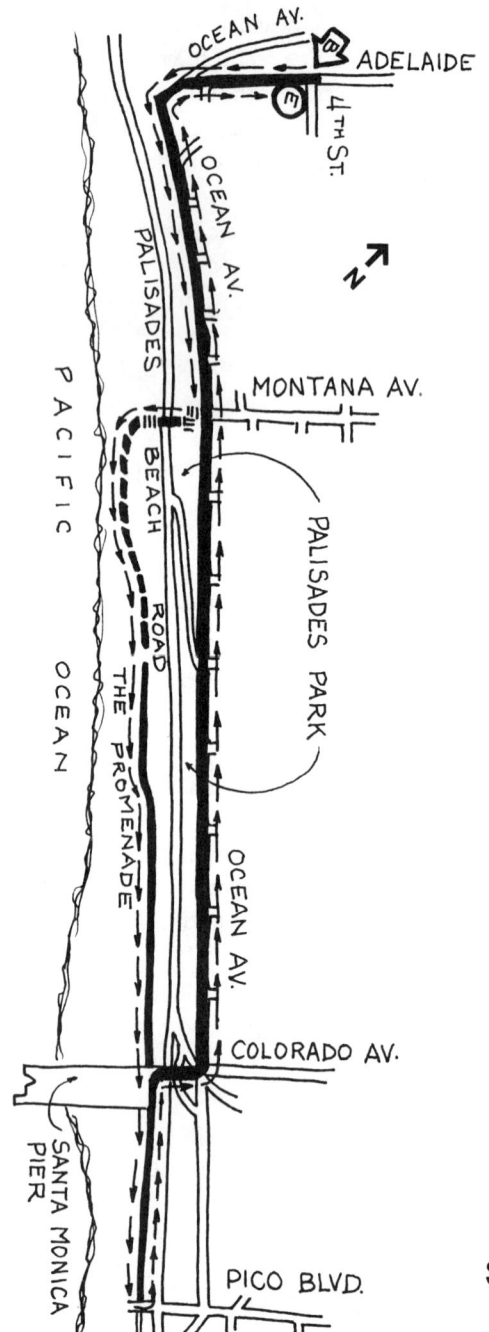

Santa Monica
(alternate)

walk on the right side of the channel, now W. Rustic Rd. Turn left. 525 has an unusual mailbox on a three-foot-high green cast-iron stand. The box has a relief design of a man on horseback blowing his horn to announce mail delivery. There is a similar mail-box in red at 507.

■ Follow the curve to the left, which becomes E. Rustic Rd. and continue on the right side of the road. The houses have footbridges across the channel to their doors.

■ Turn left on W. Channel Road. Cross to the other side of the road and turn left on Entrada. Watch for angles: six streets come together at the intersection, plus the stairway. Look for the signs: Ocean Ave (300 N.) and Entrada Dr. (400) Next to 380 Entrada is a stairway we ascend (189 steps) to Fourth and Adelaide. When we began the walk on Adelaide, we were in Santa Monica. We crossed into L.A. when we reached the lower section, but the post-office address was Santa Monica! At the top of the stairs we see the signatures of stair joggers—a half-full plastic container of Nutra Sweet Body Fuel Low Calorie Sports drink, and another one of Evian Spring Water. The joggers will pick up their traces on the return climb. Turn right on Adelaide to Ocean and to our beginning.

Notes From My Journal:
It was at the Ocean View Hotel in 1926 that Aimee Semple McPherson exchanged her street clothes for a bathing suit and strode into the Pacific Ocean, not to be heard from for six weeks.

Beach Side-trip

For those who love beach walking, the following is a 3-mile walk beginning at Fourth and Adelaide.
Rating: 1 Orange, 1 Apple

■ Turn left on Ocean Ave. and walk through Palisades Park. The sun is filtering through the leaves; people are strolling, groups of friends are sitting around the outdoor tables, talking and playing cards. Others are sitting on the grass next to their open umbrellas. The atmosphere is reminiscent of Seurat's *Picnic On The Grass*. In the rose garden is a bronze bust of Arcadia Bandini deBaker (1827-1912) descendant of the Bandini family, founders of Santa Monica. (Aside: the original Juan Bandini came from Spain in the 1700s. Through intermarriages the clan has included the Sepulvedas, the Carrillos, the Estudillos, the Machados and the Alvarados—all recipients of land grants in the Los Angeles area. Subsequently, they have contributed holdings toward the development of various towns. Currently there are 150 Bandini family members united in a limited partnership dealing in L.A. real estate.)

■ At Montana, descend the wooden stairway to the beach. It is designed in a moderate zigzag pattern and has wood-and-metal railings. Looking back and up is rewarding. Chaparral grows along the sandstone cliffs, which have vertical ridges eroded by wind and water. This pattern, repeated many times, has a monumental effect. The stairway ends approximately 20 feet above the grade of the road, at which point we connect with the skyway that stretches over the Pacific Coast Highway and comes out at the beach.

■ Walking across the skyway we see to our left a mural on an angled ruin of a retaining wall (once part of a building) of a scene of water, mountains and plants. The peaks are painted on a broken jagged section emphasizing its outline. At the end of the skyway we walk onto the stairs, beautifully designed with angled risers, which bring us down to the road and the beach. A children's playground and rest-rooms are here on the beach. Sanderlings are scurrying about looking for food.

■ Walk south to the Santa Monica pier where probably the most famous of California carousels is located. It was built in 1922, and is the only original Philadelphia Toboggan Company merry-go-round in operation on the West Coast. It has 46 horses and two carriages, and has been a leading character in *The Sting, Elmer Gantry* and many TV productions. About two blocks south of the pier was the original site of Muscle Beach, a precursor of today's parcourses, where health- and body-conscious people performed their exercises. Muscle Beach, now relocated in Venice, was celebrated in the 1948 film of the same name, directed by Irving Lerner. Two blocks farther south on the beach, near Pico, are the beginnings of the planned Natural Elements Sculpture Park, where all the sculptures will utilize wind, the sun and/or sand.

■ Return by walking north. Take the Colorado Ave. ramp up to Ocean Ave. and Palisades Park. Turn left on Ocean Ave, Then turn right on Adelaide to our beginning.

Notes From My Journal:
In the 1920s the La Monica Ballroom, which could accommodate 10,000 dancers was on the pier.

Walk 18

CASTELLAMMARE
Washout/watchout

Boundaries: Sunset Blvd., Palisades Dr., Will Rogers State Beach, Pacific Coast Hwy.
Rating: 1 Orange, 1 Peanut, 3 M&Ms

Notes From My Journal:
California has 1100 miles of Pacific Ocean coast. Living high on the cliffs above the water, Castellammare residents learn to read the cloud formations, feel the rhythm of the ocean breakers and anticipate the sunsets. In exchange for the gift of having sky and water continuously in sight, they accept the calculated risk of being subjected to periodic years of heavy rain and mudslides.

■ Our spiral walk will take us around the fragile mountain cliffs terraced with homes We will see areas that have suffered from recent mudslides; we will see beaches and views of the ocean stretching to infinity. Castellammare ("castle on the sea") is a section of Pacific Palisades, which is part of L.A.

■ Begin at Castellammare and Sunset Blvd., which is also a convenient bus stop. Follow Castellammare around the curve. A new restaurant with a total ocean view is being built on the left side of the road. Follow the curve to Stretto Way, where we see John Barrymore's former summer home at 17501 Castellammare. Just before the right turn on Posetano Road is a wondrous site—an Italian villa at 17531 Posetano. Built in 1923 of stucco and wood, it was specifically designed to duplicate an Italian villa. The roof is of red tile imported from Italy; the wooden beams, shutters

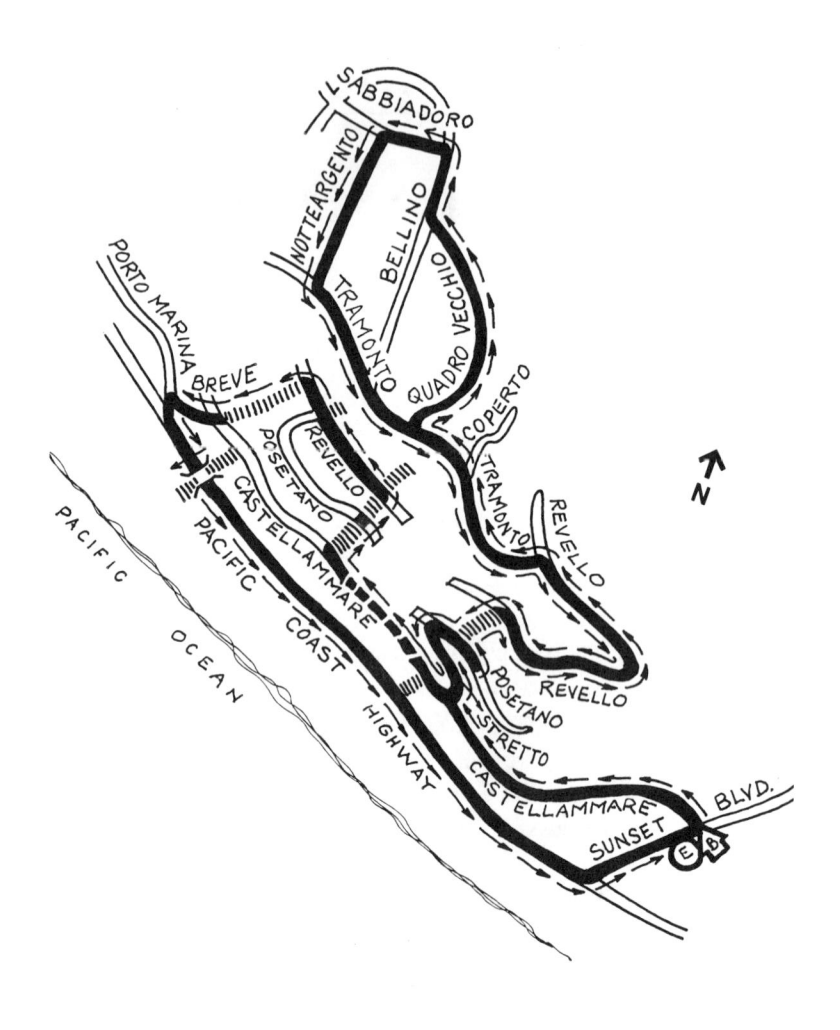

Castellammare

and doors are blue. The villa is situated on several levels; the garage, with living quarters above it, is at street level; the main house is high up on the hill at 17520 Revello, embracing a full cove view of the Pacific Ocean. The dome on top of the garage was built as an ornament by the present owner. I am not surprised to learn that the house does shift a bit—geologically speaking. The actress Thelma Todd was purportedly murdered or committed suicide here in 1935; the mystery has never been solved. Was the original owner, Roland West, the movie producer and director involved? How?

Notes From My Journal:
The first time I explored this area was in the wet year of 1982. The stairways nearby were covered by overgrown weeds among the debris from the washed-out roadbed. The most startling evidence of the mudslide was a long concrete stairway lying on its side!

■ Continuing toward the right, we talk with the owner of 17500 Posetano, a modest domicile, who tells us that the house was owned at one time by Francis X. Bushman, a well-known 'romantic star' from the World War 1 period. Walk past 17432 Posetano to see the views of the ocean and L.A.; then double back to the 1927 concrete stairway next to 17445 Posetano, which we ascend to Revello. Along the way we recognize African daisies and snapdragons. Hummingbirds are in the eucalyptus.

■ Turn right on Revello. The first house to our right, 17480, is striking in its angles and white austerity. The 36-inch-diameter drainage pipe on our left is startling by virtue of its length—approximately 70 feet! It was installed in 1969 after the destructive 1964 landslide that removed the street, destroyed the bridge and the apartment house, and damaged the sewer line. Then came years of abnormally heavy rains—1978, 1980, and 1983. The bulkhead had to be replaced in 1978 and again in 1980. A court decision ordered L.A. to restore Revello, a privately owned street. The landslides here of the 1930s were memorable, but legally it has been established that Revello, built on conglomerate bedrock, is stable.

■ The hillsides are covered with chaparral and the lupine are being rustled a bit by some lizards who venture forth into the sunshine. We pass by 17446 Revello, an unadorned glass and stucco flat-front horizontal structure built in 1963 as "Beagles House" by Pierre Koenig. Evidences of the mudslide are around us—ruts and deep ridges along the sides of the road. Weeds and Mediterranean grasses and annuals are returning to this disturbed area.

■ At the intersection of Revello and Tramonto, turn left on Tramonto. Note the fallen bluff and remnants of a house foundation across from 17543. A washout of the road has been corrected, for the time being, at the intersection of Coperto Drive (200 N.) I enjoyed the contrast of walking the area in a year of flood and in a year of drought.

■ Turn right on Quadro Vecchio Dr., then right on Bellino. Turn left on Sabbiadoro Way. Turn left on Notteargento Dr. (200 N.) and left on Tramonto (17700 W.). Pass 17630 Tramonto Dr. and be rewarded by a great ocean view.

■ Walk around the bend past Bellino (200 N.) past Coperto and turn right on Revello (17500.) This section was a washout area, but now a sign on the hillside indicates that a new home is to be built! We see and hear many birds in this area. Walk to the end of Revello Dr. to 17520, to see the front of the Italian villa. Now descend the stairway that we came up. Black-eyed susans and some of the oldest and thickest jade plants we've ever seen are on the hillside. Turn right on Posetano, then left on Stretto. Bumps in the pavement along the ocean side suggest that pilings have been driven into the hillside to stabilize it.

Ghost Stairways

Jerry Martz, a veteran walker, enjoyed designing the following long and short Castellammare addenda walks.

■ LONG VERSION: Turn right on Castellammare Dr. Cross the washout area on the footpath; walk to 17564. Turn right and ascend the stairway across from 17564. Cross Posetano Rd. and continue up the stairway to Revello Dr. Note the dead-end stairway across the street and classify it as a ghost stairway.

■ Turn left on Revello Dr. At the intersection of Revello Dr.and Posetano Rd. is another ghost stairway up the hill; and above us, cliff-hanging houses. Continue on Revello Dr. to 17717. Turn left and descend the stairway across from 17717. Cross Castellammare Dr. and follow Breve Way down the hill. Here is another ghost stairway across the street where Breve Way joins Porto Marina Way. Turn left on Porto Marina Way.

■ Bear left where Porto Marina Way joins Pacific Coast Hwy. 17575 Pacific Coast Hwy. is a curious structure (we'll have to learn more about it). Cross Pacific Coast Hwy. to the beach, via the skyway. Toilet facilities are on the beach side of the overpass. Walk southeast along the footpath.

(We stop at Gladstone's on the beach for some excellent fish.) Turn left at Sunset Blvd. to Castellammare, to our beginning.

■ SHORT VERSION: From "Turn right on Castellammare Dr." above (page 98) continue to the end of the street, crossing the washout area on the footpath. Walk to 17564 Castellammare, turn left and descend the stairway. Cross Pacific Coast Hwy. via the skyway to the beach. Turn left at Sunset Blvd. to Castellammare to our beginning.

Notes From My Journal:
Castellammare di Stabia, Castelnuovo, Castelvecchio, Castel del Piano are some of the hill towns in Italy. Each was built around a castle that provided the town's defense.

Acknowledgments

All kinds of accidental happenings inspired me to write *Stairway Walks in Los Angeles*. In 1959, I began to meet people who lived in the city, and subsequent meetings with each of them piqued my interest about Los Angeles.

What is it that is so seductive about Los Angeles? Why do these people want to live here? I visited Los Angeles to find out, and I continue to come back. There is an immense variety in people, geography and interests, and an energy that encourages new directions in the arts. I also found something special for myself: neighborhoods.

I am grateful to those writers of articles and books on California history who helped shape my ideas of Los Angeles. I thank you, Ruth Cordish, Philip Chandler, Charles Fisher, Lucille Lemon, Clarence Ross, Ed Ryerson, Siegfried Seibt, Gert and Ed Blue, and others for answering my questions about Los Angeles.

My heart-felt gratitude to my daughters: Polly Walker who arrived for a visit, found hundreds of chapter notes flying about the room, caught them, read them, snipped them, and put them in order with enviable ease; and Mimi Melody, who provided me—on my walks—with imaginary literary companions taken from her then current readings.

A special thank-you to Gene Smith, who can accurately outline any walk; to Sally Beck, the Highland Park community activist who introduced me to activists from other neighborhoods and gave me a feeling for Highland Park's past and present; friends and friends of friends who scouted out walks: Melinda Peters, Ellen Holden, Sandy Loeb, Betty Olson, Rick Gordon, Dorothy Millunchick, Jerry Fagin, Howard Solomon, Dick Clark, Lillian and Bob Burt and their friends.

I dedicate the following walks to friends who walked and rewalked problem areas and submitted valuable feedback: Highland Park, Walk 3, to Joe Stripling Jr.; South Beachwood, Walk 11, to Joan Gordon; Venice, Walk 16, to Julia Ross; Castellammare, Walk 18, to Jerry Martz.

I thank Trudie Douglas our illustrator, and Pat Beebee our cartographer. And to my best friend, Max, who participated in the entire process, a hundred thousand thanks.   —A.B.

I grew up on the top edge of the Palisades, the cliffs towering over the Hudson River. So cliffs and hills have always felt like home to me. When I moved to Los Angeles, I was pleased to discover that my reporting beat at the *Los Angeles Times* included some of the hilliest territory in L.A.: Griffith Park, Silver Lake and Echo Park. Thanks to my editors at the *Times* who first allowed me to do an article about stairways in L.A. That article brought Adah and me together.

Along the way, Alma Carlisle, an architectural historian in the city's Department of Public Works, was very helpful and, more important, enthusiastic. Leon Smith, a detective who has written books about Laurel and Hardy film locations, went well out of his way to show me how "the boys" carried that piano. Also thanks to neighborhood activists Christine O'Brien in Hollywood and Michael Heesy in Silver Lake.

I'd be remiss if I didn't mention my dog, Hudson, who exuberantly pulled me up many a step oblivious to the world's opinion of canines with pit-bull heritage. I'd also like to acknowledge the dog who lunged at me on a Silver Lake stairway the day I left Hudson home. That other dog ripped my pants but stopped before breaking flesh. Thanks for stopping, Fido.

And of course, thanks to my wife, Leda, who produced a baby faster than I finished this book.   —L.G.

Index

Abbey San Encino 19
admission of California 2
Ahmanson Theater 8
Ain, Gregory 42
Allison, David 81
Angelino Heights 31
Angelus Temple 29, 34
Arroyo Seco Park 19
Avila, Don Francisco 11

Barrymore, John 95
Beachwood Market 64
Biltmore Hotel 9
Bradbury Building 9
Bright, David 77
Browne, Clyde 19
Bunche, Ralph 77
Bunker Hill 5
Bunker Hill Steps 8, 9
Burbank, Luther 26
Bushman, Francis X. 97

California Coastal Commission 87
Chandler, Raymond 31
Chinatown 5, 11
Church of Our Lady Queen of Angels 10
Church of St. Casimir 52
Cornell, Ralph 78
Crespi, Juan 1, 4

Daniels, Mark 51
DeMille, Cecil B. 58, 67, 70
Dickson, Edward A. 75, 81
Disney studios, original 52
Disney, Walt family 8
Dodger Stadium 28, 33
Doheny, E.L. 2
Donahue, Daniel and Bernadine Murphy 51
Dorothy Chandler Pavillion 8

El Conquistador 41
El Pueblo State Historical Park 10
El Sereno Junior High School 14

Elysian Heights Elementary School 35, 36, 37
Elysian Park 1
Ennis-Brown house 53, 56

Feliz, Jose Vicente 53
Field Act 3
First Interstate World Center 8
First United Methodist Church 69
Fort Moore Pioneer Memorial 5, 7, 10, 11
Four Square Gospel Church 29
Fremont, John C. 2

Gabrieleno Indians 1
Goodhue, Bertram 8
Graham, Robert 78
Grand Central Market 9
Grauman's Chinese Theater 58
Griffith Park 28, 56, 57
Griffith Park Planetarium 57
Griffith, D.W. 70

Halprin, Lawrence 8
Heritage Square 17
Hollywood Bowl 70-71, 72, 74
Hollywood Bowl Self Storage Company 60
Hollywood Heritage 67
Hollywood Presbyterian Church 58-59
Hollywood Studio Museum 67, 69
Hollywoodland 63, 66

Immaculate Conception Home for Girls 42
Ince, Thomas 70
Isozaki, Arata 8

Janss, Edwin and Harold 80
John Marshall High School 49
Judson Glass Design Studios 19, 20

Kay, Carl 72
Kinney, Abbot 83, 87

Koenig, Pierre 97

La Perlita bakery 41
Lachaise, Gaston 77
Lake Hollywood 64
Laurel and Hardy 39
Letts, Arthur 80
Lipchitz, Jacques 77
Little Tokyo 5, 11
Long Beach earthquake 3
Los Angeles & Santa Fe Railroad 26
Los Angeles City Hall 7, 10
Los Angeles Dodgers 3
Los Angeles Hall of Records 7
Los Angeles Normal School 75
Los Angeles Philharmonic 8
Los Angeles River 7
Los Angeles Times 9, 10, 15, 21
Los Feliz School 47
Lummis, Charles Fletcher 15

Mark Taper Forum 8
Marsh, Robert 27
Martz, Jerry 98
Marvin, Lee 91
Maybeck, Bernard 51
McPherson, Aimee Semple 29
Micheltorena, Manuel 2, 41
Million Dollar Movie Theater 9
Monastery of the Angels 61-62
Moore, Dr. Ernest Carroll 75
Moore, Henry 78
Moreno, Antonio 42
Muma, Irwin 77
Muscle Beach 94
Music Center 7, 8
Musso and Frank's 58

Neutra, Dion 45
Neutra, Richard 7, 38, 43

Occidental College 17
Olio, the 41
Ord, Lt. Edward O.C. 2
Owens Valley 2
Ozzie Dots 41

Pacific Electric Railway 2, 19

Pacific Palisades, 95
Pershing Square 9
Phoenix bakery 33
Pico House 11
Pico, Pio 2
Porter, Edwin S. 70
Portola, Gaspar de 1
Powell, Lawrence Clark 81
Protection of the Holy Virgin
  Russian Orthodox Church 60

San Fernando Valley 2
Santa Monica Mountains National
  Recreation Area 89
Schindler, R.M. 38, 41 69
Seafood Bay restaurant 41
Self-Realization Fellowship 26, 27
Selig, William 70
Sepulveda, Dona Vicente 1
Sequoyah League 15
Simon, Norton 77
Sisters of the Immaculate Heart of
  Mary 51
Smith, Gene 51
Smith, Jack 21
Southwest Museum 15, 17, 23
St. Athanasias Episcopal Church 31
Swanson, Gloria 3

Todd, Thelma 97
Tsutakawa, George 78

Union Station 7, 11
University of California 75

Vedanta Society of Southern
  California 60, 61
Voulkos, Peter, 78

Watts racial riot 3
Weissmuller, Johnny 91
Wells Fargo Court 8
Wilcox, Harvey 70
Wilson, Benjamin D. 23
Wright, Frank Lloyd 53, 56, 72

Yogananda, Paramahansa 26